GOVERNANCE.COM

Visions of Governance in the 21st Century

Why People Don't Trust Government
Joseph Nye Jr., Philip Zelikow, and David King, editors
(1997)

Governance in a Globalizing World
Joseph S. Nye Jr. and John D. Donahue, editors
(2000)

Governance amid Bigger, Better Markets
John D. Donahue and Joseph S. Nye Jr., editors
(2001)

GOVERNANCE.COM: DEMOCRACY IN THE INFORMATION AGE

Elaine Ciulla Kamarck

Joseph S. Nye Jr.

Editors

VISIONS OF GOVERNANCE
IN THE 21ST CENTURY
Cambridge, Massachusetts

BROOKINGS INSTITUTION PRESS
Washington, D.C.

Library of Congress Cataloging-in-Publication data

Governance.com : democracy in the information age / Elaine Ciulla Kamarck and Joseph S. Nye, Jr., editors ; Visions of Governance in the 21st Century.
    p.   cm.
  ISBN 0-8157-0216-7 (cloth: alk. paper)
  ISBN 0-8157-0217-5 (pbk: alk. paper)
  1. Information society—Political aspects—United States. 2. Information technology—Political aspects—United States. 3. Internet—Political aspects—United States. 4. Political participation—United States—Computer network resources. 5. United States—Politics and government—2001—Computer network resources. I. Kamarck, Elaine Ciulla. II. Nye, Joseph S. III. Visions of Governance in the 21st Century (Program)
  JK468.A8 G643 2002
  320.973'0285—dc21   2001007473

9 8 7 6 5 4 3 2 1

The paper used in this publication meets minimum requirements of the American National Standard for Information Sciences—Permanence of Paper for Printed Library Materials: ANSI Z39.48-1992.

Typeset in Adobe Garamond

Composition by Cynthia Stock
Silver Spring, Maryland

Printed by R. R. Donnelley and Sons
Harrisonburg, Virginia

Contents

Preface

THIS VOLUME ORIGINATED with Visions of Governance for the Twenty-first Century, a project of the John F. Kennedy School of Government at Harvard University. The project began in 1996 amid concern that as the twentieth century drew to an end, democratic governance was losing the support of the governed. Declining trust in government, perceived and actual performance deficits in government, and a sense that, as President Bill Clinton said in his 1996 State of the Union address, "the era of big government is over" led to a decision by Dean Joseph S. Nye Jr. to devote several years of study to the future of governance.

The first volume generated by this project, *Why People Don't Trust Government*, examines the scope and performance of government and the possible causes of citizens' dissatisfaction with government. Following publication of that study, a group of faculty met to identify the factors that were forcing major changes in the form and functions of government. We identified three—information technology, globalization, and marketization—and built the research agenda of the Visions of Governance project around them. Although these three factors are interrelated—information technology, for instance, has been a critical factor in globalization, as it has been in the spread of markets—we decided to deal with each factor independently, so that we could manage our inquiries more systematically. In addition to the book *Why People Don't Trust Government*, this project has resulted in a systematic study of globalization called *Governance in a Globalizing World* and a book on markets called *Governance amid Bigger, Better Markets*.

In 1998 a group of scholars, drawn largely but not exclusively from the Kennedy School faculty, were asked to examine different pieces of the governance puzzle—representation, community, politics, bureaucracy, international relations—using the revolution in information technology as an independent variable. In other words, how was information technology affecting traditional, time-honored institutions and concepts of governance? People who were experts in areas of governance and familiar with information technology produced an initial volume of essays called *Democracy.com?*

The current volume, the fourth in the Visions of Governance series, builds on, expands, and updates that initial volume. It offers a balanced and sometimes skeptical look at the transformations that the information revolution is making (or not making) in our basic institutions and processes of governance. Joe Nye begins with an essay that places the information revolution in historical context and in the context of the other major forces—globalization and marketization—that are contributing to significant changes in governance around the world. He outlines a series of hypotheses about how the "third industrial revolution" is likely to impact politics and government and looks at the effects of these factors on the diffusion of governance from supranational to subnational and from private to public to third sector.

This introductory essay is followed by Arthur Applbaum's speculations on the nature of deliberative or Madisonian democracy in the information age. In the next chapter, in one of the livelier responses from beyond the grave, James Madison himself (a.k.a. Dennis Thompson), @founding.gov, then ruminates on the ability of the new technologies to mitigate the effects of faction.

William Galston's essay on the impact of the Internet on civic life frames the debate about whether there can be such a thing as community on the Internet by outlining four criteria for evaluating community. The essay poses the provocative possibility that the Internet could intensify current tendencies toward fragmentation and polarization in American civic life.

The next section of this volume contains three essays on politics. In "Revolution, What Revolution?" Pippa Norris employs data on Internet usage from the Pew Research Center for the People and the Press to investigate the nature of citizen activism on the Internet and to explore online political activism. She asks whether the Internet will expand political participation and serve to mobilize new activists or will simply reinforce the participation of those who are traditionally political activists. Her essay is followed by Elaine Kamarck's comparison of the use of the Internet as a campaign tool in the 1998 and 2000 elections. This essay examines Internet campaigning in a historical context and looks at the way many candidates used the Internet, what they were attempting to accomplish, and the limits and potential of the Internet as a new campaign tool. If these two essays are grounded in data on the present, the final essay in this section, by David King, takes us into the future. It suggests how a hypothetical congressional candidate might use the power of the Internet to construct a congressional campaign.

The section on politics is followed by two essays on bureaucracy. Jane Fountain's essay argues that a useful starting point for a theory of information-based bureaucracy can be found in the core concepts of traditional bureaucracy—command and control. The second essay in this section, by Jerry Mechling, raises some crucial questions about the future of electronic government with regard to the reengineering of government processes and with regard to electronic money, in particular. In the final essay in this volume, Joseph S. Nye Jr. and Robert Keohane discuss the implications of the information revolution for world politics—in particular, the notion that "the information revolution creates a new politics of credibility in which transparency will increasingly be a power asset."

These essays are meant to provoke thought and further research about the ways in which the information revolution is transforming our institutions of governance. Some exhibit a healthy skepticism toward those who would read too much into the effects of the information revolution. Yet all the authors recognize its significance and attempt to articulate what the information revolution may mean for governance in the future. As such it is hoped that these essays will offer an important window on the challenges and promises of twenty-first-century government.

In addition to the many faculty members of the Kennedy School of Government who commented on these chapters, the authors would like to thank the following: Pippa Norris is most grateful to Andrew Kohut and the Pew Research Center for the People and the Press for generous release of the survey data on online users. The main surveys are those of online users in 1995, 1996, and 1998, the May 1998 survey of the public's media consumption, the November 1998 preelection and postelection surveys, and the October to November 2000 surveys. For details see www.people-press.org. Elaine Ciulla Kamarck thanks her assistant, Lynn Akin, for coordinating the original research for this chapter. Jerry Mechling thanks those who gave comments or otherwise assisted in drafting this paper including David Barber, Scot Barg, Teresa Cader, Jack Donahue, Sandra Hackman, Fred Hayes, Norm Jacknis, Bob Knisely, Mark Moore, Richard Sobel, Kimberly Spragg, Zach Tumin, Jim Van Wert, Charles Vincent, Jim Vollman, and Irene Yarmak. Support for these essays has been generously provided by the Pew Charitable Trusts, the Stratford Foundation, and Oracle. Special thanks are owed to Christopher Kelaher and Janet Walker, of the Brookings Institution Press; Katherine Kimball, copy editor; Inge Lockwood, proofreader; Julia Petrakis, indexer; Jack Donahue, director of the Visions of Governance in the Twenty-first Century project; and Lynn Akin, project coordinator.

GOVERNANCE.COM

1

JOSEPH S. NYE JR.

Information Technology and Democratic Governance

PUBLIC CONFIDENCE IN government has declined over the past few decades in a large number of democratic countries.[1] The causes are complex. Some see the decline, at least in the United States, as a return to a deeply ingrained American suspicion of concentrated power after expectations about government rose to unrealistic heights in the aftermath of success in World War II.[2] Others see it as a result of a long-term shift toward postindustrial values that emphasize the individual over the community and diminish respect for authority and institutions.[3] Still others see it as a reaction against the centralization of government in the twentieth century that saw the federal budget grow from 3 percent of gross national product in 1929 to 20 percent in the past two decades. Some analysts argue that centralized government, unlike private enterprise, has not yet adapted to the changes being wrought by the "third industrial revolution."[4]

Historical Analogies

In the first industrial revolution around the turn of the nineteenth century, the application of steam to mills and transportation had a powerful effect on the economy, society, and eventually government. Patterns of production, work, living conditions, social class, and political power were transformed.

Public education arose, as literate trained workers were needed for increasingly complex and potentially dangerous factories. Police forces such as London's "bobbies" were created to deal with urbanization. Subsidies were provided for the necessary infrastructure of canals and railroads.[5] In what is sometimes called the second industrial revolution, around the turn of the twentieth century, electricity, synthetics, and the internal combustion engine brought similar economic and social changes. The United States, for example, went from being a predominantly agrarian to a primarily industrial and urban nation. In the 1890s most Americans still worked on farms or as servants. A few decades later, the majority lived in cities and worked in factories.[6] Social class and political cleavages were altered. Once again, with lags, the role of government changed. The bipartisan Progressive movement ushered in antitrust legislation, early consumer protection regulation by the forerunner of the Food and Drug Administration, and economic stabilization by the Federal Reserve Board.[7] In what some have called the third industrial revolution, at the turn of the twenty-first century, the impact of computers and communications technology on the economy and society should eventually produce analogous major changes in the functions of government.

A number of criticisms of such grand analogies can be raised. At a semantic level, the term *industrial revolution* is not totally appropriate for what is sometimes called a postindustrial phenomenon. Daniel Bell, for example, argues that the term mistakenly conflates the introduction of steam power as a form of energy and the creation of factories, which are social organizations. He prefers to refer to three great technological revolutions, with the current one marked by electronics, miniaturization by transistors, digitalization, and software.[8] In addition, "revolution," defined as a disjunction of power, is often difficult to discern except in retrospect. Moreover, historians differ on the dating and duration of earlier industrial revolutions. The term was not coined until 1886, a century after the first industrial era began.[9] Although there may have been discontinuities in technological progress, with new leading sectors in each era, it has been difficult to prove the existence of long waves or cycles of economic growth. Efforts to specify exact timing of Eric Kondratieff's or Joseph Schumpeter's cycles of technological change have not been successful.[10] Finally, one must be wary of technological determinism.[11] Technology affects society and government, but the causal arrows work in both directions. Technological change creates new challenges and opportunities for social and political organization, but the response to those challenges depends on history, culture, institutions, and paths already taken or forgone.

Nonetheless, with appropriate caveats and caution, the historical analogies can help suggest hypotheses and avenues for exploration. Abrupt changes often occur after a long buildup, and punctuation points can often be found. Analysts need not fall into the fallacy of technological determinism to see that technology is one of the significant causes of social and political change. As Bell argues,

> Since the techno-economic changes pose 'control' problems for the political order, we find that the older social structures are cracking because political scales of sovereignty and authority do not match the economic scale. In many areas we have more and more economic integration and political fragmentation. . . . If there is a single overriding sociological problem in post-industrial society—particularly in the management of transition—it is the management of scale.[12]

Centralization or Diffusion?

Six decades ago, the eminent sociologist William Ogburn cited technology as one factor in his prediction of greater political centralization. In 1937 he argued that "government in the United States will probably tend toward greater centralization because of the airplane, the bus, the truck, the Diesel engine, the radio, the telephone, and the various uses to which the wire and wireless may be placed. The same inventions operate to influence industries to spread across state lines. . . . The centralizing tendency of government seems to be world-wide, wherever modern transportation and communication exist."[13]

By and large, Ogburn was right about his next half century, but will this continue to be true in the twenty-first century? President Bill Clinton and other politicians proclaimed that the era of big government is over, but they have said little about what will take its place. Is the basic premise correct—and if so, is it correct for all dimensions of democratic government? If this is the case, what are the causes and how reversible are they?

Questions of appropriate degrees of centralization of government are not new. As Charles Kindleberger points out, "How the line should be altered at a given time—toward or away from the center—can stay unresolved for

Figure 1-1. *The Diffusion of Governance in the Twenty-First Century*

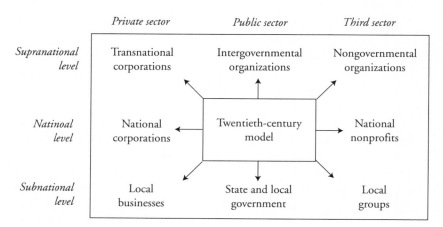

long periods, typically fraught with tension."[14] If Bell and others are correct that the nation-state has "become too small for the big problems of life and too big for the small problems,"[15] we may find not centralization or decentralization but rather a diffusion of governance activities in several directions at the same time. Some functions may migrate to a supragovernmental or transnational level, and some may devolve to local units. Other aspects of governance may migrate to the private sector. The matrix presented in figure 1-1 lays out the possible diffusion of activities away from central governments, vertically to other levels of government and horizontally to market and private nonmarket actors—the so-called third sector. The matrix is simply a map of the possible dimensions of the locus of collective activities. It can be combined with a hypothesis that the twentieth century saw a predominance of centripetal forces and that the next period may see a greater role of centrifugal forces.

There is some evidence of diffusion. For example, between 1962 and 1995, federal civilian employment in the United States saw a net growth of 15 percent, while state and local employment grew by 150 percent.[16] As a share of gross national product, federal expenditures (excluding transfers) have fallen, while state and local expenditures have increased.[17] In the past two decades, privatization has transferred a number of functions out of the public sector in a large number of countries.[18] Nonprofit organizations are playing an increasingly large role in the United States, where after two decades of proliferation they represent almost 7 percent of all paid employment.[19] International nongovernmental organizations have multiplied tenfold over the past two decades and have increased their influence on a number of issues.[20] Transgovernmental networks of bureaucrats and judicial officials have expanded in autonomy and number, with the effect of disaggregating the state for certain policy issues.[21] The transnational domains of international production set limits on national welfare measures, and many functions such as credit ratings and arbitration of disputes are handled largely in the private transnational sector.[22] International security, the ultimate function of the state, now involves defense against transnational actors as a primary threat.

On the other hand, the overall trends are far from clear. Some issues show centralization, some decentralization, and some show both at the same time. For example, in the area of personal security, there has been an enormous increase in privatization of security forces. In 1970 there were one-and-a-half times as many private as public security personnel; by 1996 that factor had doubled.[23] Nonetheless, the early 1990s witnessed a demand for federalization at the same time, suggesting a rise in the demand for several types of governance in response to a perception of rising crime. Even after the privatizations of state-owned enterprises in the 1980s, the share of national income spent by the state in the wealthy democratic countries averaged 46 percent.[24] Moreover, countries vary: In contrast with Europe, total government spending has held steady in the United States and Japan, at around a third of the economy, and has declined in New Zealand.[25] Some states are weaker than the private forces within them; others are not. Panama, Sierra Leone, and Haiti are different from Brazil, South Africa, and Singapore. The trends from external forces feel stronger for European states than they do for the American superpower. In short, the jury is still out, and it is not clear how strong the trends toward decentralization will be in an information age. More work needs to be done in refining the dependent variable and understanding the implications for democratic governance, as well as analyzing the strength of the causes that could be leading to diffusion.

Three Trends

Three independent but interrelated current trends give credence to the prospect that the new century may see a shift in the locus of collective activities away from central governments. These are globalization, marketization, and the information revolution.

Globalization refers to the increase in the scale and speed of flows of goods, people, and ideas across borders, with the effect of decreasing the effects of distance. It is not new.[26] Globalization increased rapidly in the nineteenth century and during the first decades of the twentieth but was curtailed, at least in its economic dimensions, from the early 1930s through the end of World War II. Globalization preceded the information revolution but has been greatly enhanced by it. In its recent incarnation, globalization can, in part, be traced back to American strategy after World War II and the desire to create an open international economy to forestall another depression and to balance Soviet power and contain communism. The institutional framework and political pressures for opening markets were a product of American power and policy, but they were reinforced by developments in the technology of transportation and communications, which made it increasingly costly for states to turn away from global market forces. Raymond Vernon argues that nearly half of all industrial output is produced by multinational enterprises whose strategic decisions on the location of production now have a powerful effect on domestic economies and wage structures, even in the absence of international trade.[27] At the same time, as Dani Rodrik points out, globalization still has a long way to go, and its post–World War II progress in democratic countries has been concomitant with the development of the welfare state in what John Ruggie calls "embedded liberalism."[28] A failure of that social contract in the democracies or a financial crisis turning into a world depression might revive protectionism, but predictions to that effect have proved wrong for the past three decades. Meanwhile, globalization constrains states' ability to levy taxes and maintain lavish benefits, and it opens opportunities for private transnational actors to establish standards and strategies that strongly affect public policies that were once the domain of central governments.

Marketization is part of globalization and, like it, has been enhanced by the information revolution, but it also has an independent domestic aspect and independent origins. Susan Strange argues that the balance between states and markets has shifted since the 1970s in a way that makes the state just one source of authority among several and that leaves "a yawning hole of non-authority or ungovernance."[29] She argues that power has diffused from governments to markets in such critical functions as maintaining the value of the currency, choosing the form of the economy, taxation, and providing infrastructure, countercyclical policy, and protection from crime.

This can be debated, as we have seen, by citing the fact that government spending as a percentage of gross national product remains above 40 percent in a number of major European countries. Even such states as Sweden and France, however, not to mention eastern Europe and the less economically developed countries, have seen significant privatizations and expansion of market forces in the past two decades. The causes of marketization are complex. They include the failure of planned economies to adapt to the information revolution, the inflation that followed the oil crises of the 1970s, the early success of the East Asian economies, and changes in political and ideological coalitions inside wealthy democracies. The net effect, however, is to accelerate the diffusion of power away from governments to private actors.

Information revolution refers to the dramatic decrease in the costs of computers and communications and the effects that has on the economy and society. According to Jeremy Greenwood, the price of a new computer has dropped by 19 percent a year since 1954, and information technologies have risen from 7 percent to about 50 percent of new investment.[30] Information technology has been responsible for a quarter of U.S. growth over the past five boom years and makes up 8 percent of gross domestic product.[31] Microprocessors have doubled computing power every eighteen to twenty-four months, and computing power now costs less than 1 percent of what it did in 1970.[32] As late as 1980, phone calls over copper wire could carry information at the rate of one page a second; today a thin strand of optical fiber can transmit ninety thousand volumes in a second.[33] The growth in Internet use has been extraordinary, with traffic increasing by 100 percent every year, versus less than 10 percent for the voice network.[34] The effect has been the virtual erasing of costs of communicating over distance.

As with steam in the late eighteenth century and electricity in the late nineteenth, there have been lags in productivity growth as society learns to fully use the new technologies.[35] Social organization changes more slowly than technology. For example, the electric motor was invented in 1881, but it was nearly four decades before Henry Ford pioneered the reorganization of factories to take full advantage of electric power. Computers today account for 2 percent of America's total capital stock, but "add in all the equipment used for gathering, processing, and transmitting information, and the total accounts for 12% of America's capital stock, exactly the same as the railways at the peak of their development in the late 19th century. . . . Three-quarters of all computers are used in the service sector such as finance and health, where output is notoriously hard to measure."[36] Whether in reorganization or measurement, it is generally agreed that we are still in the early stages in the current information revolution.

Political Effects of the Information Revolution

Critics correctly point out that the current period is not the first to be strongly affected by changes in the technology and flows of information. Johannes Gutenberg's invention of movable type, which allowed printing of the Bible and its accessibility to large portions of the European population, is often credited with playing a major role in the onset of the Reformation. The advent of truly mass communications and broadcasting a century ago, which was facilitated by newly cheap electricity, might be considered a second information revolution. It ushered in the age of mass popular culture.[37] The effects of mass communication and broadcasting, though not the telephone, tended to have a number of centralizing political effects. Although information was more widespread, it was also more centrally influenced, even in democratic countries, than in the age of the local press. Franklin D. Roosevelt's use of radio in the 1930s is a case in point. These effects were particularly pronounced in countries with totalitarian governments, which were able to suppress competing sources of information. Indeed, some theorists believe that totalitarianism could not have been possible without the mass communications that accompanied the second industrial revolution.[38] On the other hand, as films, cassettes, and faxes proliferated, the later technologies of the second information revolution helped to undermine governmental efforts at information autarky. The overall effects were not always democratizing. In some cases, such as Iran, the technologies of the second information revolution merely changed the nature of the autocracy.

At one stage, it was believed that the computers and communications technology of the third information revolution would also have the effect of further enhancing central governmental control. George Orwell's vision of 1984 was widely feared. Mainframe computers seemed set to enhance central planning and increase the surveillance powers of those at the top of a pyramid of control. State-controlled television would dominate information flows. Even today, through central databases and by removing the gray areas of noncompliance, computers can enhance some central government functions, and privacy issues remain an important concern. Some aspects of surveillance have become cheaper and easier. Nonetheless, on balance the prevalent current view is closer to Ithiel de Sola Pool's description of "technologies of freedom."[39]

As computing power has decreased in cost and computers have shrunk in size and become more widely distributed, their decentralizing effects have outweighed their centralizing effects. Moreover, the marriage of computers and communications technology that has evolved into the Internet creates a system with few central nodal points and with a robust capacity in case of a central failure. Power over information is much more widely shared. Central surveillance is possible, but governments that aspire to control information flows through control of the Internet face high costs and ultimate frustration. Rather than reinforcing centralization and bureaucracy, the new information technologies have tended to foster network organizations, new types of community, and demands for different roles for government. By changing how we work, they change our social attitudes and political behavior.

Morley Winograd and Dudley Buffa argue that the extensive corporate work pyramid dominated by centralized commands divided management and the working class, white-collar and unionized blue-collar workers.[40] This pyramid dominated the political process and strongly influenced the evolution of government in the second industrial revolution that shaped the twentieth century. Now, they argue, new information technologies are again reorganizing work. Speed, agility, and customization are the best ways to produce value in the consumer marketplace. Large bureaucratic pyramids turn out to be a less effective way to organize such work than are networks within and between firms. The knowledge workers who staff network organizations see themselves neither as labor nor as capital. To earn the loyalty of their employees, both companies and governments must appeal to them in new ways. They want government to have the convenience and flexibility of the marketplace. The result may be a transformation of politics and, more slowly, of government.

Information technology may affect politics and collective action in a number of other ways. First, information technology reinforces global production strategies and markets with the constraining effects on governmental action already noted. Second, it decreases the relative importance of commodities and territory, which makes geographic distance less important. This in turn has an effect on the communities that underlie political action. Third, the Internet makes borders more porous and jurisdiction less important. Fourth, information technology is changing the nature of banks and money in a way that will make both taxation and central control of monetary policy more difficult. The exponential rates of technological change and the shortening of product cycles make it difficult for governmental institutions and regulations to keep up. More information and shorter news cycles mean less time for deliberation before response. Fifth, some virtual communities may develop interests and power independent of geography. In some countries the Internet may enhance both local and transnational communities more than national community. Sixth, the demise of broadcasting and the rise of narrowcasting may fragment the sense of community and legitimacy that underpins central governments. Seventh, educational patterns will change, and the greater agility of younger generations with the new technologies may further erode deference to age, authority, and existing institutions.

Obviously, these hypotheses about the information revolution are not the only possible sources of change in the locus and quality of governance activities in the twenty-first century. We have already shown that globalization and marketization, though closely related to and enhanced by the information revolution, have autonomous causes. Moreover, there are strong cultural institutional and political forces that are particular to each country. Race, for example, has had a strong effect in American history: decentralizing before 1865; centralizing during Reconstruction; decentralizing before World War II; centralizing shortly after the war; perhaps decentralizing since the defection of the South from the Democratic coalition after 1970. Immigration and ethnic diversity may have a decentralizing effect, though that has been a recurrent and sometimes exaggerated concern in American history. The current demographic trends toward older populations with their entitlements may have a centralizing effect. Although there may be changes at the margin, the entitlement philosophy of the welfare state remains strong. A variety of forces tug the locus of collective activity in different directions, and in different ways on different issues and in different countries. Nonetheless, it seems plausible to look closely at the hypothesis that the three new interrelated trends, and particularly the information revolution (or whatever other label), will have a stronger net effect of diffusion.

Although there is evidence to support the effects of these three trends, it would be a mistake to believe that such effects are irreversible. Technology is only one factor in a complex set of social causes. We should also ask what conditions these trends depend upon and what it would take to slow, derail, or reverse them. For example, would a strong and prolonged economic downturn lead to demands for government response that would alter marketization and globalization? Will "grand terrorism" on the scale of the World Trade Center attacks lead to a demand for intrusive government even at the cost of civil liberties?[41] Would the increasing power of states such as China, India, or a revived Russia—particularly if accompanied by an expansionist ideology—transform the international system so that the defense functions of government would return to the cold-war model? Could ecological trends such as global warming become so clear and alarming that the public would demand much stronger governmental action? Such scenarios are worth exploring both as contingencies and counterfactual thought experiments to check our reasoning about the strength of the new causes. On the other hand, barring such low-probability but high-impact events, a trend toward diffusion of governance activities seems plausible.

The effects on central governments of the third information revolution are still in their early stages. The dispersal of information means that power is more distributed and networks tend to undercut the monopoly of traditional bureaucracy. The speed or instantaneity of Internet time means that all governments, whether central or local, have less control of their agendas. This may make all government more difficult, as there will be fewer degrees of freedom for political leaders to enjoy before they must respond to events. Changes in the nature of money, the disintermediation of banks, and the diminished ability to identify and collect taxes may particularly reduce central governmental capacity. More privatization and public-private partnerships may be a response. Horizontal shifts on the matrix outlined earlier in this chapter may outweigh vertical changes. All government bureaucracy may become flatter and more service oriented. Moreover, though government may become flatter, governance may nonetheless become more complex. At this stage, however, all of the foregoing is speculation.

Similar changes may occur in the political processes of democracy—what might be considered the input rather than the output side of government. One can imagine both a better and a worse political world resulting from the impact of the third information revolution. In a bleak vision of the future, one can imagine a thin democracy in which deliberation has greatly diminished. Citizens will use the set-top boxes on their Internet televisions to engage in frequent plebiscites that will be poorly understood and easily manipulated behind the scenes. The growth of thin direct democracy will lead to a further weakening of institutions. In addition, political community will be fragmented by the replacement of broadcasting by narrowcasting. Broadcasting may have often produced a lowest common denominator, but at least something was common. In the new world, each community will "know" only its own perspective. The prospects for deliberative democracy as outlined in the Federalist Papers will look dim.

Alternatively, one can envisage a better political process in the future. New virtual communities will cross-cut geographic communities, both supplementing and reinforcing local community. In Madisonian terms the extensive republic of balancing factions will be enhanced. Access to information will be plentiful and cheap for all citizens. Political participation, including voting, can be made easier. The low costs of contact and contract will reduce the costs of participation. The Internet may end the hegemony of broadcast television that has undercut political parties and made the process of politics extremely costly in terms of the funds that must be raised. Just as television came to dominate campaigns some four decades ago, the Internet may come to dominate the political process in the decades to come. Access to the political process will be easier and cheaper. Again, both of these futures are highly speculative at this point. Technology alone will not produce one or the other outcome. Much will depend on other political choices.

Political Choices

"This is the second age of democracy," argues British prime minister Tony Blair. "The first was the vote, getting the basic decent standard delivered and pensions, housing, and all the rest of it, but people want choice today, and people want freedom to do things differently at [the] local level, to have better and more innovative ways of deciding their own priorities."[42] Information technology has the capacity to make such a world possible, but it will not happen automatically. As collective activities diffuse across the space described by the matrix outlined in this chapter, there will be important implications for democratic governance. The European Union extols the principle of "subsidiarity" or deciding issues at the lowest possible level as a means of bringing government closer to the people. In the American federal system, public opinion polls show that local and state governments enjoy somewhat higher levels of public trust than does the central government.[43]

In principle, devolution and subsidiarity seem to enhance democratic governance, but as James Madison pointed out two centuries ago, local communities with dominant factions are more likely to suffer from a tyranny of the majority. In American history, for example, central government interventions in the states were essential for the democratic enfranchisement of African American citizens. Moreover, as some actors become more mobile across state and national jurisdictions, local government tax bases erode and burdens are shifted onto the shoulder of those who are relatively immobile, which often means those who are poor.[44] The unstructured development of information technology may increase inequality and accentuate gaps between the haves and the have-nots. Information technology may enhance life choices for some people while diminishing it for others.

A strong libertarian tendency among many enthusiasts of information technology assumes that the growing perfection of markets through the Internet will solve the problems of democratic governance. They believe that as more and more activities shift horizontally on the matrix in this chapter, the role of government will diminish. Microcontracting will allow people to make their own choices on an ever increasing range of issues. It is true that markets enhance choice, but they provide more choices for those who can enter the game with a large pile of chips than for those who cannot.

Aside from the question of inequality of opportunity, there is also a question of public spaces and public goods.[45] Public goods are nonexclusive and nonrivalrous. Once produced, no one can be excluded from their consumption, and one person's consumption does not diminish that of others. Lighthouses have been a classic example used in economics textbooks. Today's technology, however, makes it possible to construct a lighthouse (or a navigational satellite) whose signal can be made available to some users and not to others. This ability to exclude lays the basis for a private market relationship and diminishes one of government's traditional roles, the provision of public goods. Highways, including the information highway, can be turned into toll roads. Indeed, one can imagine a situation in which information technology produces automated pricing systems that privatize all public spaces such as roads and parks. Alternatively, one can imagine deliberate government actions to preserve public spaces and to widen the access to information technology across social and organizational barriers. Such policies could encourage the use of the Internet as an adjunct rather than a substitute for face-to-face relations in reinforcing civic involvement.

Similarly, one can imagine alternative choices in the governance of cyber-space. As Lawrence Lessig argues, software and hardware codes and archi-tecture constitute cyberspace. They imbed political values that have con-stitutional importance. Yet "they are private and therefore outside the scope of constitutional review."[46]

In short, we are only in the early stages of this latest information revo-lution. As in earlier periods of industrial revolution, public responses to technology are lagging behind private ones. Some aspects of that lag are fortuitous, but some are not. The future of democratic governance depends upon improving our ability to make the relevant distinctions.

Notes

1. Joseph Nye, "The Decline of Confidence in Government," introduction to Joseph S. Nye Jr., Philip D. Zelikow, and David C. King, eds., *Why People Don't Trust Government* (Harvard University Press, 1997), pp. 1–2; Pippa Norris, ed., *Critical Citizens: Global Support for Democratic Government* (Oxford University Press, 1999).

2. See, for example, Robert Samuelson, *The Good Life and Its Discontents: The American Dream in the Age of Entitlement, 1945–1995* (Vintage, 1995).

3. Ronald Inglehart, "Postmaterialist Values and the Erosion of Institutional Authority," in Nye, Zelikow, and King, *Why People Don't Trust Government,* pp. 217–36.

4. See, for example, Peter Drucker, "The Next Information Revolution," *Forbes,* August 24, 1998, pp. 46–58; Alvin Toffler and Heidi Toffler, *The Politics of the Third Wave* (Kansas City, Mo.: Andrews and McMeel, 1995); Morley Winograd and Dudley Buffa, *Taking Control: Politics in the Information Age* (Henry Holt, 1996); Don Tapscott, *The Digital Economy: Promise and Peril in the Age of Networked Intelligence* (McGraw-Hill, 1996).

5. David S. Landes, *The Unbound Prometheus: Technological Change and Industrial Development in Western Europe from 1750 to the Present* (Cambridge University Press, 1969), chaps. 2–3; David Thomson, *England in the Nineteenth Century, 1815–1914* (Viking Penguin, 1978), pp. 63–68; Alfred Chandler Jr., *The Visible Hand: The Managerial Revolution in American Business* (Harvard University Press, Belknap Press, 1977), pp. 90–91.

6. Zane L. Miller, *The Urbanization of Modern America: A Brief History,* 2d ed. (San Diego: Harcourt Brace Jovanovitch, 1987), passim.

7. Stuart W. Bruchey, *Growth of the Modern American Economy* (New York: Dodd Meade, 1975); Thomas McCraw, *Prophets of Regulation: Charles Francis Adams, Louis D. Brandeis, James M. Landis, Alfred E. Kahn* (Harvard University Press, Belknap Press, 1984), chaps. 1–5.

8. Daniel Bell, foreword to *The Coming of Post-Industrial Society: A Venture in Social Forecasting* (Basic Books, 1999), p. 8.

9. Ibid., p. 5.

10. Nathan Rosenberg, *Exploring the Black Box: Technology, Economics, and History* (Cambridge University Press, 1994), chap. 4 .

11. See Anthony G. Oettinger, "Information Technologies, Governance, and Government: Some Insights from History," paper presented at the 1998 Visions in Governance Conference at Bretton Woods, sponsored by the Kennedy School of Government, Harvard University, July 19–22, 1998 (www.ksg.edu/visions/conferences/brettonwoods3/oettinger95.ppt [October 15, 2001]).

12. Bell, *The Coming of Post-Industrial Society,* pp. 94, 97.

13. William Fielding Ogburn, "The Influence of Inventions on American Social Institutions in the Future," *American Journal of Sociology,* vol. 43 (November 1937), p. 370.

14. Charles P. Kindleberger, *Centralization versus Pluralism* (Copenhagen: Copenhagen Business School Press, 1996), p. 13.

15. Bell, *The Coming of Post-Industrial Society,* p. 94.

16. John D. Donahue, *Disunited States* (Basic Books, 1997), p. 11.

17. Ibid., pp. 9–11.

18. Daniel Yergin and Joseph Stanislaw, *The Commanding Heights: The Battle between Government and the Marketplace That Is Remaking the Modern World* (Simon and Schuster, 1998); Susan Strange, *States and Markets,* 2d ed. (New York: Pinter, 1994), pp. 14, 73.

19. *Nonprofit Almanac, 1996–97* (San Francisco: Jossey-Bass, 1996), p. 29.

20. Jessica T. Mathews, "Power Shift," *Foreign Affairs,* vol. 76, no. 1 (1997), pp. 50–66; Marc Lindenberg, "Declining State Capacity, Voluntarism, and the Globalization of the Not-for-Profit Sector," *Nonprofit and Voluntary Sector Quarterly,* vol. 28, no. 4 (1999), supplement, pp. 147–68.

21. Anne-Marie Slaughter, "The Real New World Order," *Foreign Affairs,* vol. 76, no. 5 (1997), pp. 183–97; see also Robert Keohane and Joseph S. Nye Jr., "Transgovernmental Relations and World Politics," *World Politics,* vol. 27 (October 1974), pp. 39–62.

22. Deborah Spar and Jeffrey J. Bussgang, "Ruling the Net," *Harvard Business Review* (May–June 1996), pp. 125–33; Saskia Sassen, *Globalization and Its Discontents* (New York: New Press, 1998), p. 16.

23. "Policing for Profit: Welcome to the New World of Private Security," *Economist,* April 19, 1997, pp. 21–24.

24. "The Visible Hand," *Economist,* September 20, 1997, pp. 17–18.

25. Organization for Economic Cooperation and Development, "General Government Total Outlays," *OECD Economic Outlook,* vol. 68 (December 2000), statistical annex, table 28, p. 236.

26. David Held and Anthony McGrew, eds., *The Global Transformations Reader: An Introduction to the Globalization Debate* (Cambridge: Polity Press, 2000).

27. Raymond Vernon, *In the Hurricane's Eye: The Troubled Prospects of Multinational Enterprises* (Harvard University Press, 1998), chaps. 1–2.

28. Dani Rodrik, *Has Globalization Gone too Far?* (Washington: Institute for International Economics, 1997), p. 65; John Ruggie, "At Home Abroad, Abroad at Home: International Liberalization and Domestic Stability in the New World Economy," *Millennium: Journal of International Studies,* vol. 24, no. 3 (1995), pp. 507–26, p. 508.

29. Susan Strange, *The Retreat of the State* (Cambridge University Press, 1996), p. 14.

30. Jeremy Greenwood, *The Third Industrial Revolution: Technology, Productivity, and Income Inequality* (Washington: American Enterprise Institute Press, 1997), pp. 20–23.

31. "Electronic Commerce Helps to Fuel U.S. Growth," *Financial Times* (London), April 16, 1998, p. 5.

32. Intel cofounder Gordon Moore formulated his now-famous "Moore's law" of microprocessing power and cost in 1965. As Intel's website essay on Moore's law notes, "The average price of a transistor has fallen by six orders of magnitude due to microprocessor development. This is unprecedented in world history; no other manufactured item has decreased in cost so far, so fast" (developer.intel.com/update/archive/issue2/focus.htm#ONE [October 15, 2001]).

33. U.S. Department of Commerce, *The Emerging Digital Economy*, chap. 1, "The Digital Revolution" (www.doc.gov/ecommerce/danc1.htm [October 15, 2001]).

34. K. G. Coffman and Andrew Odlyzko, "The Size and Growth of the Internet," *First Monday: Peer-Reviewed Journal on the Internet*, vol. 3 (October 1998) (www.firstmonday.dk/issues/issue3_10/coffman/index.html [October 15, 2001]).

35. Douglass North, *Structure and Change in Economic History* (W. W. Norton), pp. 163–64.

36. "Productivity: Lost in Cyberspace," *Economist*, September 13, 1997, p. 72.

37. See, for example, Drucker, "The Next Information Revolution"; Neal M. Rosendorf, "El Caudillo and American Pop Culture: How Postwar Franco Spain Attempted to Use Hollywood, U.S. Tourism, and Madison Avenue for Its Own Political and Economic Ends," Ph.D. diss., Harvard University, 2001, chap. 1.

38. Carl F. Friedrich and Zbigniew Brzezinski, *Totalitarian Dictatorship and Autocracy*, 2d ed. (Harvard University Press, 1965).

39. Ithiel de Sola Pool, *Technologies of Freedom* (Harvard University Press, Belknap Press, 1983).

40. Winograd and Buffa, *Taking Control: Politics in the Information Age*.

41. Ashton Carter, John Deutch, and Philip Zelikow, "Catastrophic Terrorism: Tackling the New Danger," *Foreign Affairs*, vol. 77, no. 6 (1998), pp. 80–94.

42. Quoted in "Undivided Loyalties: FT Interview with Tony Blair," *Financial Times* (London), January 14, 1999.

43. Nye, "The Decline of Confidence in Government," passim; David W. Moore, "Public Trust in Federal Government Remains High," Gallup News Service, January 8, 1999 (www.gallup.com/poll/releases/pr990108.asp [October 18, 2001]).

44. Donahue, *Disunited States*.

45. Deborah L. Spar, "The Public Face of Cyberspace: The Internet as a Public Good," in Inge Kaul, Isabelle Grunberg, and Marc A. Stern, eds., *Global Public Goods: International Cooperation in the Twenty-first Century"* (Oxford University Press, 1999).

46. Lawrence Lessig, "Cyber-Governance," *CPSR Newsletter*, vol. 16 (Fall 1998), p. 4.

2

ARTHUR ISAK APPLBAUM

Failure in the Cybermarketplace of Ideas

THE YEAR TWO THOUSAND BUG has struck hard. I don't mean the dreaded glitch in the date function of computers but a parallel phenomenon—the tendency of otherwise perfectly sober commentators to get giddy in the face of a very, very round number. We have a great need to make history tidy by naming and dating epochs, and the temptation now to prognosticate revolutionary, indeed, millenary change is great. So when asked to write about the effects of the information revolution on the ideal of Madisonian democracy, my first reaction was skeptical and contrarian. That very day, however, I received an unsolicited e-mail spam with the following quotations:

—"This 'telephone' has too many shortcomings to be seriously considered as a means of communication. The device is inherently of no value to us."—Western Union internal memo, 1876

—"Heavier-than-air flying machines are impossible."—Lord Kelvin, president, Royal Society, 1895

—"Everything that can be invented has been invented."—Charles H. Duell, commissioner, U.S. Office of Patents, 1899

—"Who the hell wants to hear actors talk?"—H. M. Warner, Warner Brothers, 1927

—"Stocks have reached what looks like a permanently high plateau."—Irving Fisher, professor of economics, Yale University, 1929

—"I think there is a world market for maybe five computers."—
Thomas Watson, chairman of IBM, 1943

—"I have traveled the length and breadth of this country and talked
with the best people, and I can assure you that data processing is a fad that
won't last out the year."—The editor in charge of business books for
Prentice Hall, 1957

—"We don't like their sound, and guitar music is on the way out."—
Decca Recording Company, rejecting the Beatles, 1962

—"There is no reason anyone would want a computer in their
home."—Ken Olson, president, chairman, and founder of Digital Equipment Corporation, 1977

—"640K ought to be enough for anybody."—Bill Gates, chairman and
founder of Microsoft, 1981

We have all chuckled over such lists before. The fortuitous arrival of this
one cured me right away of my smugness. It also started me thinking about
how new the new information technologies really are. Although uninvited,
the joke got my attention. I knew who passed it along but not where it had
originated or how many thousands had seen it before, or how many muta-
tions it had undergone before turning up in my mailbox. I do not and cannot know if the lines are accurate or libelous. I can, however, with a quick
cut and paste, pass them along to you, and so I do, with the meagerest of
disclaimers. Lord Kelvin cannot help looking foolish, but Bill Gates can,
whether or not his quote is accurate. He can make himself out to be as
visionary as he wants to be and praise himself quickly, cheaply, and anonymously to millions. Alternatively, he can attack his enemies. Soon enough
he will be able to send a customized message that has been found to be
effective in influencing the opinions of people who match your demographic characteristics, surf your favorite websites, subscribe to your
favorite magazines, rent your favorite videos, and take your favorite med-
ications. There are smallish companies that own more mainframes than
Tom Watson thought would ever be built, and in their databases are details
about all your credit-card transactions, for starters.

If you are a financial analyst or large investor who follows such companies, you are invited to participate in quarterly interactive teleconference
calls with the chief executive officer. The company gets to decide who is a
member of this club, and small shareholders are not. If you are listening,
the company knows who you are, because you signed up for the call.
Unless you ask a question, however, no one else on the call knows that you
are listening. Sometimes the first question is a slow pitch down the middle

from a bullish, friendly analyst. If companies are screening tougher questioners, no one would know. The particular rules of this game could have been very different, because the technology allows many variants. Some options have been physically ruled out by the particular path along which teleconferencing technology has developed—two callers probably cannot, through this system, easily connect with each other for a private conversation while the main call is going on. If there were enough demand for such a variant, however, someone would design it. The identities of callers could be known to all, to none, or to a select few; all could hear the same message or different messages; control over who can say what when to whom can be allocated in many ways. The Securities and Exchange Commission might have a say in this, but the basic technological capability exists.

The only prognostication about the new cyberdemocracy technologies offered in this chapter is a rough sketch of what is possible given the existing basic technological capabilities. Possible does not mean likely, and much of what I suggest will never come to pass, either because there will not be enough demand or because industry standards will close some options or because paths will be blocked by regulation or social custom. The most visible capability is the vastly expanded possibilities for interactive communication: fast, cheap, and round-the-clock access to thousands of news sources, political chat rooms, electronic town halls, and millions of individualized pitches from politician to citizen and back again. Much of this will be junk, of course, and new technical and institutional ways to search, filter, verify, and identify will emerge. The dominant gatekeepers could be centralized, vesting a lot of power in either existing or new media organizations and content providers; or they could be "intelligent agents" that automatically search and filter, identify and block identification, under the direction of users. Predictably, there also will be new ways to grab your attention despite the filtering mechanisms. Some interactive communication will be shallow, and some deep. James Fishkin has pioneered the deliberative poll, in which a representative sample of Americans are brought together for a weekend to discuss issues and then render their opinions. The new technologies will greatly lower the cost and increase the frequency of such encounters.

This is the face of cyberdemocracy that we are now starting to see, but there are three other background capabilities of perhaps even greater importance: vastly expanded capacities for data collection, for computation, and for automation. The "record" of politicians and public officials could explode with detail, with every word and move, promise and vote tracked over many years. So could the record of citizens: their every purchase, membership, donation, plane ticket, speeding ticket, and account balance. Much of this already exists in far-flung commercial databases, and whatever barriers to consolidation and access may exist are not technical. Politicians will have greatly expanded profiles of citizens by district, neighborhood, block, or individual. When a private citizen enters the public arena, his or her individual file will be in great demand by reporters and opponents. We should not forget, however, that alongside all this rapidly expanding political intelligence will be rapidly expanding policy intelligence: data-intensive policy areas such as the economy, health care, social policy, and the environment will be awash in information.

The capacity to crunch all this data will mushroom. The policy wonks will know more and be able to say more with more confidence, and so will the political junkies. Fed by nonstop, real-time opinion polling, endless market testing of messages and images, and instant and cheap online focus groups, no social scientist need ever again go hungry. More complex simulations with better and better models will be run on alternate political strategies. Look for midcourse corrections on the teleprompter. Better political analysis will generate greater refinements in narrowcast political communications. Your buttons will be found and pushed.

Voters will not only be able to follow in great detail what their elected representatives are doing, they will also be able to exert more direct influence. There are no technical barriers to establishing online auctions trading campaign contributions for legislative action, perhaps mediated by advocacy groups, perhaps made up of thousands and thousands of small contingent bids, settled automatically upon performance. Before each roll call, senators will see on screen the opportunity cost of independence. What can be done with money in the coffer can also be done with votes at the poll. If voting online is possible, so is advance voting. Advocacy groups could deliver the votes of their members midterm in exchange for important legislation. Just about any market that can be imagined can be implemented online, and anything implemented online can be automated, like stock market program trading, to take action on your behalf in response to a precipitating event. Of course, no physical constraint will prevent citizens from making law and policy directly in electronic assemblies that could always be in session.

These possible technology-driven innovations, some more fantastic than others, can be sorted along two dimensions: one, call it directness, measures the effect of the innovation on the power of constituents relative to their elected representatives; the other, call it deliberativeness, measures the effect of the innovation on the quality of public discussion. Information-based innovations fit in all four quadrants. Some favor the professional politicians by giving them more refined ways to manage and manipulate public opinion and voter behavior at the polls, and some deliver to citizens a greatly expanded capacity to monitor public officials, register views, contribute funds, extract commitments, or govern themselves. Some promote demagogic pandering and others promote know-nothing populism; some lead to enlightened statesmanship and others to reasoned and responsible citizen participation. All in all, a move to any quadrant is possible, and to say much more about what in fact will happen over the coming decades is to engage in pure speculation.

Much can be said, however, about what we should want to happen and, insofar as we can influence what happens, what we should aim at. We can evaluate moves toward more or less direct and more or less deliberative democracy, though to do so we need to take (and defend) a stand on one of the central questions of political philosophy: how can we rule one another legitimately? I argue for an unpopular view of democratic legitimacy—but it is part of the view that its correctness does not depend on how many people hold it. If you think I am mistaken, I invite you to offer (and defend) another view. No serious assessment of cyberdemocracy, however, can proceed without doing some political philosophy first.

Legitimacy

The argument goes something like this: among the highest human values is the freedom to rule oneself. But living in society requires mutual limitations on our freedom—law is coercive. The puzzle of collective self-rule is how to justify to one another this mutual coercion. The unjustified exercise of political coercion is simply tyrannical, so we must explain why we are not tyrants to one another. We are not if, in exercising collective rule, we treat one another as moral equals. Treating another as a moral equal in this context requires, among other things, that we recognize that we each have a valid claim to a fair share of control over how we collectively rule ourselves. To secure that claim, we are each entitled to a fully adequate scheme of political liberties consistent with equally adequate political liberties for everyone else.[1] If we deprive others of the equal political liberties, we deprive them of their fair share of collective self-rule, and so we tyrannize them. Simply put, what justifies mutual political coercion is the realization and protection of the equal political liberties.

Treatment of one another as moral equals does not require equal treatment. There are morally relevant reasons for treating persons in different circumstances differently. In the distribution of resources, differences in need or in merit might be morally relevant reasons. In the restriction of freedoms, differences in past violation of or future threat to the liberty of others, or differences in our obligations to others, might be morally relevant reasons. For some to exercise political coercion over others for a morally irrelevant reason, however, is to act illegitimately. Some reasons for my coercing others are always illegitimate: because I am being paid to do so; because it will enrich my sister-in-law; because it will benefit my tribe; because I hate them; because God wills it. When questions of justice are in the balance, legitimacy requires that proposals for legislation appeal to a conception of justice, to what we owe one another, and not to self-interest or to the interests of the many.

If reasons for depriving others of liberty can be illegitimate, then the test of legitimate collective self-rule is in part substantive and not purely formal or procedural. Legislative majorities elected properly under fair procedures can still act illegitimately, and so tyrannically. They do so most clearly when they deprive a minority of the equal political liberties for irrelevant reasons and so fail to treat all citizens as moral equals. The guarantee of at least some political liberties is a conceptual or practical precondition of legitimate democratic rule. No regime that disenfranchises, silences, or enslaves a minority counts as a legitimate democracy. This is why the constraints on majoritarian lawmaking imposed by a bill of rights make a constitutional democracy more, not less, legitimate than a regime with no constraints on majority rule. For the same reason, a representative democracy is more, not less, legitimate than a direct democracy if it does a better job of protecting political freedom.

Where does the political participation of citizens fit in this view? The equal political liberties include the right to an equal vote in free and fair elections, equal protection under law, freedom of thought and discussion, the right to petition, assemble, and organize, the right to be informed about government activities, and—to give these liberties fair value—the right to a decent education, among other things. In short, we treat one another as moral equals when we provide for each other the freedom to exercise a fair share of political control without fear or favor, as long as doing so does not deprive others of their liberties.

A reasonably informed voter who freely chooses not to participate more actively in politics is not for that reason less free, nor is the government for that reason more tyrannical and less legitimate. There are reasons to be a passive citizen that are consistent with collective self-rule: an informed voter may have confidence in her elected representatives to advance her interests in ways consistent with justice and legitimacy, she may be satisfied with the way things are, and she may have other valuable projects and commitments that demand her time and attention. There might be circumstances under which a passive citizen wrongly free rides on active citizens and so fails in her obligations to the rest of us; but she does not fail to be free. Moreover, the circumstances of wrongful free riding must be carefully specified. Hiring someone to do a job for you ordinarily does not involve free riding.

The claim that the greater participation of all entails the greater freedom of all suffers from a fallacy of composition. True, if coercive government were more responsive to my will, I would be more free. I cannot tyrannize myself. However, it does not follow that if the government were more responsive to the will of the majority we would all be more free, because we can—and do—tyrannize one another. There is nothing to the view that direct democracy is intrinsically more legitimate than representative and constitutional democracy.

It is often claimed that checks on the will of the majority, such as representative government and judicial review, are paternalistic and thereby disrespectful to a competent and mature people. It is paternalistic to restrict your liberty to keep you from harming yourself; it is not paternalistic to restrict your liberty to keep you from harming others. Constitutional constraints on majoritarianism aim at the second, not the first, and it is a dangerous romanticism to suppose, in the United States today, that "we the people" need more protection from "them the government" than from one another. Unjustly treated minorities can be forgiven if they reject a reified account of "we" under which their injuries are self-inflicted.

Where does deliberation fit in this view? First, we have to say something about what is meant by the term. Just about every form and venue of political communication has, at one time or another, been claimed as a part of a deliberative process, from New England town meetings to election campaign smear tactics and everything in between. If we take the widest definition, democratic deliberation is any practice of interactive communication in which actors in a democracy seek to affect the decisions of one another by influencing beliefs about politically relevant facts, values, concepts, or interests.

Note that this does not rule out deceptive and manipulative political communication. An actor need only seek to affect another's politically relevant belief, not necessarily in the direction of beliefs that are true or believed by that actor to be true. Broad as it is, this preliminary definition is incompatible with views of politics that take interests and values to be known and fixed, as some models of interest group pluralism have done. Also, broad as this is, it does not cover all political activity. Not all political acts seek to influence belief: some acts aim at affecting the decisions of others through the provision of incentives and disincentives, and some acts aim at forcing or coercing others. Many political activities are complex, in that they contain both deliberative and nondeliberative aspects. A negotiator, for example, might seek to affect another's decisions in all three ways: by influencing beliefs, by offering incentives, and by coercively worsening or threatening to worsen the other party's alternative to agreement. Some political activities are efficacious precisely because of an ambiguity in whether or not they operate deliberatively: most politicians do not want to view campaign contributions as legalized bribery.

Of course, the sort of deliberation advocated by proponents of deliberative democracy is much more noble than this. They mean something like a reflective process of honestly giving and listening to reasons and arguments among persons who are open to changing their views about facts, interests, and values for the right reasons and who have the capacity and the motivation to imaginatively occupy the perspectives of others. As have most academics, I have committed my life to that sort of deliberation, and of course I wish there were more of it in democratic politics.

If the concept of deliberation is to be useful in assessing the design of political institutions, however, rather than simply as a pious exhortation, it cannot be defined by the quality of the motivations of participants any more than it can be defined by the quality of the outcomes. We can dictate neither. A usable definition of deliberative democracy encompasses processes and institutions that aim at changing motivations, and consequently outcomes, for the better. So, as I use the term, what makes the Supreme Court a deliberative institution is not that its members are fair, impartial, and honest. We hope that they are, but we cannot make them so. Rather, the Court is deliberative in that its practices include hearing arguments, discussing cases, taking its time, and giving reasons in opinions; the institution attempts to screen out improper motives by granting justices lifetime tenure and by having rules about ex parte contact and conflict of interest.

For any actual deliberative process, we want to know how good it is at drawing out from participants better motives and more reasoned changes in view. Because no process will wholly succeed, we also want to know how robust the process is to cheaters and incompetents. Good, just, and legitimate political outcomes might better be served by avoiding a deliberative process that is not sufficiently strategy-proof or foolproof. This is not to say that one should not offer reasons. Treating our fellow citizens as moral equals worthy of respect requires both that we restrict their liberty or set back their interests only with good reason and that, generally, we give them those reasons and consider their objections in return. On the other hand, if we have the formal legal authority to unilaterally decide a matter, we surely are not required to defer to the outcome of a deliberation conducted in bad faith. One must resist, here and elsewhere, the temptation to compare the ideal form of one's favored institutional arrangement with realized instantiations of the disfavored alternatives.

When it comes to deliberation, this temptation is especially great because it is easy to confuse the enterprise of designing actual legitimate institutions with the enterprise of modeling the principles of morality or of justice as the outcome of a hypothetical deliberation conducted by idealized persons under idealized conditions. I think some version of the constructivist moral theories of Immanuel Kant, John Rawls, T. M. Scanlon, and Jürgen Habermas is correct, but it does not follow that we should try to mimic in our real institutions the devices they employ to model unanimous agreement under the conditions of freedom, equality, and reasonableness. No real deliberative process can succeed in eliminating background inequalities in bargaining power or in motivating participants not to exploit the advantages that such inequalities confer; no real deliberative process will leave participants equally and fully informed; no real deliberative process can ensure that all are moved to seek agreement on terms that all can reasonably accept.

If any real deliberative process of any size resulted in unanimity, we would first turn for an explanation to duress or fraud, rather than sweet reason; and when real deliberations are not unanimous, we do not suppose that the dissenters are being unreasonable. Surely we should encourage deliberative processes to shape the views of citizens if the alternative is for their opinions to be formed by superficial sound bites, uniformed prejudice, and unreflective self-interest. There is no reason to suppose, however, that the unconstrained rule of deliberating majorities is a more legitimate solution to the puzzle of collective self-rule than a system with constitutional constraints on majoritarianism. Think of all the provisions and interpretations of the U.S. Constitution that, in your view, properly protect basic liberties, along with those provisions that you believe are mistakes. Now suppose you have a choice: you can either keep the Constitution as it is or substitute representative samples of the American people who will periodically meet for a month or more and deliberate about what our basic liberties are and how they should be protected. Under which scheme are you more secure against tyranny? Deliberation is a fine thing, but when it comes to preventing tyranny, one does not remove the belt when one adds the suspenders.

Madison

And so, we come to Madison. It is a bit misleading to speak of the ideal of Madisonian democracy, since James Madison is the great theorist of the nonideal. He framed institutions, to borrow a phrase from Jean-Jacques Rousseau, for men as they are. This does not mean that we cannot construct normative principles that Madison could endorse—that is what I have been doing; rather, it means that for Madison, facts about the nature of politics require us to be pessimistic about realizing a normative ideal. Madison's world is always second-best.

Madison understood that normative principles of political philosophy and pragmatic prescriptions for the design of political institutions are connected by enduring facts about human nature: men are not angels, one cannot judge one's own cause without bias, passions and interests give rise to faction, and factions are prone to tyrannize. Because the causes of faction cannot be removed without also destroying liberty—a prescient observation—his institutional prescription is to control the effects of faction. Representation, separation of powers, and an extended republic of sufficient size will diminish the chances that any one faction will gain a majority or be able to act in unison. In short, the great evil is tyranny, the cause is faction, and the solution is an institutional design that deters the formation of majority factions by making ambition counteract ambition and mediates passion through representation.

Does the arrival of the new information technologies call for a revision in the Madisonian account? Surely it does not change the normative principle. Liberty is no less important, tyranny is no less wrong. Do the infor-mation technologies change the facts about the nature of politics that cause factional interests and passions? One might object that Madison's view is too dismal (though I do not). However, if we grant, arguendo, that he was right about the deep causes of faction before the advent of the Internet, the new technologies do not mitigate the causes, which are self-love and pas-sion. Note that Madison does not argue that faction is caused by lack of information or expertise, which the vast resources of the information rev-olution could cure. Neither partisan interests nor collective passions are brought on by ignorance. "Had every Athenian citizen been a Socrates; every Athenian assembly would still have been a mob."[2] So the problem to which representative democracy is the solution is not bad information—lack of expertise, narrow bandwidth, informational complexity or over-load. The problem is bad will—factional interests or inflamed passions, the defect of the better motive. Representation as a remedy for deficiencies in information or expertise is John Stuart Mill's argument, not Madison's.

Do the new technologies change the effects of faction? If Madison is right about the importance of the extended republic as a check against the mischiefs of faction, then there is cause to worry. The extended republic provides two safeguards: greater numbers multiply interests, making it less likely that a majority will have a common interest in oppressing a minor-ity, and geographic spread makes it harder for factions to recognize their strength and organize for action. The Internet does not shrink the number of interests, but precisely those aspects of interactive communication that thrill the direct democrats make the identification and organization of fac-tious majorities more likely.

It is by now obvious that, for Madison, the logistical difficulties of direct democracy and mass political participation are not at all a regrettable cir-cumstance that necessitate representation as a poorer substitute. It is Edmund Burke who offers the logistical circumstance as a justification for legislative independence: "Government and legislation are matters of rea-son and judgment, and not of inclination; and what sort of reason is that, in which the determination precedes the discussion; in which one set of men deliberate, and another decide; and where those who form the con-clusion are perhaps three hundred miles distant from those who hear the arguments?"[3] If presented with the modern electronic remedies that could have covered the three hundred miles and allowed his constituents to instruct him after parliamentary deliberation, Burke no doubt would fall back on his other reasons for legislative independence. Madison, on the other hand, has no need to retreat. For him, distance and difficulty of communication are to be celebrated as checks on majorities in their own right, and he can only lament the electronic contraction of the extended republic.

The upshot of information technology on the effectiveness of representation in deterring faction is harder to assess: innovations in all of the basic capabilities—communication, data collection, computation, and automation—make representatives more accountable to politically active citizens. Voters and contributors will have a greatly expanded capability to follow the legislator's record, to gain access, and to make credible threats and promises about support. Legislative independence is self-defeating if independent legislators are swiftly replaced by more deferential ones. Cyberdemocrats welcome the prospect of mimicking direct democracy by tightening control on representatives. Whether direct democracy or direct oligarchy is mimicked depends on the numbers and distribution of active citizens; and whether this is good or bad for the protection of liberty depends on the interests and passions of the electronically active.

The elected official looking for elbow room will also have new tools to employ. Market-tested, narrowcast political communication could be effective in attracting and keeping the more passive voters. If the Internet brings more manipulatory politics, the advantage is likely to go to the professionals. If we suppose instead that the deliberationists succeed in getting a rich and thoughtful conversation going, it is unclear whether this will result, on balance, in more legislators' being reeducated by the majority of their constituents or in more legislators' successfully explaining their positions or winning room for discretionary judgment. The rise of deliberation might just select for a different kind of candidate with different oratorical skills— but we should all keep our day jobs.

Equilibrium

Why has the possibility of direct electronic democracy generated more enthusiasm than dread? The prospect of large numbers, speed, iteration, and complexity that information technology offers triggers appealing images of equilibrating mechanisms. We, of course, know that not all equilibria are good. Natural equilibria can be catastrophic—ask the dinosaurs—and social equilibria unjust—look at segregated housing. However, the temptation to analogize from the favorable equilibria of prosperous economic markets and beautiful old-growth forests to any complex system is strong. So David Johnson, the director of the Aspen Institute's Internet Policy Project, can believe this: "Drawing on recent research at the Santa Fe Institute and elsewhere that holds that any complex system, whether technological or biological, will spontaneously order itself, Mr. Johnson predicts that the Internet will produce its own social order—one that, because it arises from the network itself, will have its own legitimacy."[4] Johnson no doubt has more to say on this than the *New York Times* reports, but surely more must be said before we accept the Panglossian claim that spontaneous ordering is good, just, or legitimate. Remember Lord of the Flies?

An appeal to the good consequences of an equilibrating process assumes both a mechanism and conditions under which the mechanism will lead to a favorable equilibrium. The mechanism must be described, and the conditions under which good results obtain must be specified. For example, general equilibrium theory in economics describes a pricing mechanism in which producers and consumers bid, and states the conditions of perfect competition that must hold, for the price system to yield efficient allocations in the production and consumption of goods: a large number of firms free to enter and exit, frictionless market transactions, costlessly enforceable contracts, markets for capital, risk, and information, and the like. This obviously is an idealization that will never be met by an actual economy, and economic theory goes on to describe the equilibria that can be expected when these conditions are only partly satisfied. For example, in the well-known "lemons" problem, George Akerlof shows how, under certain conditions, information asymmetries can lead to the unraveling of a used-car market, so that no buyer is willing to buy any car that a seller is willing to sell, even though there may be clear gains to trade.[5]

Similarly, if factual claims for the good effects on the democratic process of the new information technologies are to be taken seriously, the conditions that must hold for the good results to occur must be specified, along with an account of how robust good results are to the relaxation of some of these conditions. This has never been done for the suggestively named but poorly specified marketplace of ideas, so we do not know if the hyperactivity of an electronic marketplace of ideas will be better or worse.

Consider Oliver Wendell Holmes's much-quoted celebration of the marketplace of ideas in his *Abrams* v. *United States* dissent:

When men have realized that time has upset many fighting faiths, they may come to believe even more than they believe the very foundations of their own conduct that the ultimate good desired is better reached by free trade in ideas—that the best test of truth is the power of the thought to get itself accepted in the competition of the market, and that truth is the only ground upon which their wishes safely can be carried out. That at any rate is the theory of our Constitution. It is an experiment, as all life is an experiment.[6]

Now, this is false in two ways. If the Constitution has a theorist, it is James Madison, and Madison would never endorse Holmes's test of truth. He needed no procedural test to pick out injustice and illegitimacy. Nor should he have endorsed the test, because Holmes is making either the false empirical claim that even deceptive and manipulative political communication leads to a convergence of belief on the truth or the false philosophical claim that truth just is whatever we think it is after we are all talked out.

Madison invokes his own equilibrium mechanism, but it is a more modest and so more plausible one. Under a separation of powers, opposite and rival interests are to supply the defect of better motives and check one another's tyrannical tendencies. It is more modest, because Madison does not predict confidently that great good, such as truth, will come from defective motives; rather his aim is to prevent a great bad tyranny, and he is not entirely confident that he will succeed. It is a serious misreading of Madison to attribute to him the view that, with divided and representative institutions in place, better motives are unnecessary, let alone counterproductive.

Conclusion

I have argued that democratic legitimacy is in part a substantive notion: to be legitimate, a government must protect its minorities from majority tyranny, and what counts as tyranny is not up to the majority. No democratic procedure alone can solve the puzzle of legitimate political coercion. Therefore, in evaluating various changes to the directness of the democratic process and the levels of political participation that information technology might bring about, we cannot simply deduce the answer from our view of some procedural ideal: direct democracy is more legitimate, the Internet is direct, therefore the Internet increases legitimacy. Rather, we must look to the effects these technological innovations will have on realizing, protecting, or violating the equal political liberties.

American government now fails at realizing political freedom in some serious ways: the current system of campaign financing amounts to legalized corruption; equality before the law is beyond the reach of most Americans because lawyers are; millions of schoolchildren fail to develop the most basic capacities for self-rule. Information technology is not going to remedy these faults, even if every poor kid does get a laptop, as Newt Gingrich once suggested. The Internet might make campaign financing worse.

What information technology will do, in ways that are difficult to predict, is create new powerful gatekeepers, increase the ease of political organization and participation for some (but not all) citizens, and give politicians much more sophisticated tools for political analysis and communication. How this will alter the balance between passion and reason, factional interest and the public interest, majorities and minorities, constituents and representatives is at this point simply guesswork. If I had to predict, I would bet on the professional pols, and I am enough of a Madisonian to root for them too.

Notes

1. See John Rawls, *Political Liberalism* (Columbia University Press, 1991), p. 5.

2. James Madison, *Federalist* no. 55, in Philip B. Kurland and Ralph Lerner, eds., *The Founders' Constitution,* vol. 1 (University of Chicago Press, 1987), pp. 407–8.

3. Edmund Burke, "Speech to the Electors of Bristol," in Kurland and Lerner, *The Founders' Constitution,* pp. 391–92.

4. Amy Harmon, "We, the People of the Internet," *New York Times,* 29 June 1998, p. D1.

5. George A. Akerlof, "The Market for Lemons: Quality, Uncertainty, and the Market Mechanism," *Quarterly Journal of Economics,* vol. 84 (August 1970), pp. 488–500.

6. 250 US 616, 630 (1919).

3

DENNIS THOMPSON

James Madison on Cyberdemocracy

To: "Arthur Applbaum" <arthur_applbaum@ksg.harvard.edu>
From: "James Madison" <jmadison@founding.gov>
bcc: "Thomas Jefferson" <tjeff@monticello.org>, "Publius" <dennis_thompson@harvard.edu>
Subject: cyberdemocracy

Message Text

Your recent paper on the implications of information technologies for Madisonian democracy has come to my attention. I do not usually deign to respond to the surfeit of messages I receive each week purporting to determine "what Madison would have said." Indeed, I receive so much spam that I have installed a filter utility that blocks, inter alia, all messages containing "Hamilton," "Anti-Federalist," and "the War of 1812."

Sources for quoted material are as follows: James Madison, *The Federalist,* ed. Benjamin Fletcher Wright (Harvard University Press, 1961), nos. 10 and 51; Robert A. Dahl, *A Preface to Democratic Theory* (University of Chicago Press, 1963), p. 146; Matt Drudge, Address before the National Press Club, June 2, 1998 (www.frontpagemag.com/archives/drudge/drudge.htm [October 15, 2001]); and Amy Gutmann and Dennis Thompson, *Democracy and Disagreement* (Harvard University Press, 1996).

Nevertheless, I am compelled to respond to your essay because of its extraordinary combination of truth and error. You come closer than any writer I have read to representing accurately my views about the new technologies, but for that reason the consequence of your errors more urgently stand in need of correction.

You are certainly correct in perceiving that the new technologies are not a panacea for the ills of American democracy and that they may even exacerbate its already perilous condition. (I have abandoned all hope of persuading anyone to employ the proper term, "republic," especially now that I have seen the uses to which the so-called Republicans have put its cognates.) The Internet undoubtedly provides more information to more people than has ever before been possible and by means of this service certainly effects a positive contribution. Who could dispute that it is better that citizens and their representatives be more rather than less informed?

As you perspicaciously observe, however, the most severe source of troubles lies not in the dearth of information but in the lack of good will—in (one might say) "the defect of the better motive." The motive of tyranny—the desire to rule over others without regard to their liberty—is deleterious in any democracy, and by diminishing the effects of geographic dispersion, the Internet removes one of the chief impediments to the formation of the tyrannical factions.

I wish to acknowledge that in my previous writings I dwelt excessively on the danger of *majority* factions. (I regret to observe that you follow me in this error.) Tyranny, I would still affirm, is a serious problem, but its threat, I now see more clearly, derives less from any well-organized majority than from temporary and shifting combinations of minorities. In support of this proposition, I appeal to the authority of a distinguished political scientist, Robert Dahl, who though laboring in a less reputable institution than yours redeemed himself by devoting nearly a whole book to discussing the Madisonian theory of democracy. Professor Dahl concludes his insightful work thus: "The making of governmental decisions is not a majestic march of great majorities. . . . It is the steady appeasement of relatively small groups."

Professor Dahl also remarks that this consequence would please me "enormously," but I should concur only if the "minorities rule" he so aptly describes is not itself tyrannical. At the risk of sounding like my friend Mr. Jefferson, I should say that as I observe the practice of American democracy today, I detect more than a few instances in which privileged minorities combine (be they corporations or professions) to thwart the will of the people.

The inference to which we are brought is that any faction, whether majority or minority, may seek to rule tyrannically, and when it does so it will find the new technologies a useful means to further its baneful ends. The Internet offers potent means by which to overcome the geographic barriers that I had hoped would help keep factious combinations from executing their schemes of oppression.

If you are correct in emphasizing this danger, you are mistaken in neglecting the possibilities that the Internet offers to check its effects. First of all, you should recall that to prevent factious combinations from endangering republics I rely not only on the "extent of territory" but also on "the greater variety of parties and interests." Under these circumstances the agreement required to sustain robust combinations is to be less often expected. "Communication is always checked by distrust in proportion to the number whose concurrence is necessary." In the chat rooms and on the bulletin boards across America, diversity of opinion is great, but the frequency of concurrence is small. The more regularly that citizens have a chance to express themselves, the less reliably they will be able to forge agreement and form stable coalitions.

The second attribute of the new technologies that may help constrain the political effects of factions is somewhat paradoxical. The ease of communication itself assists citizens all too well in finding compatriots who share their interests, however particular and even eccentric these interests may be. In my leisure time (which I now possess in greater quantities than previously), I confess that I have from time to time found myself surfing the net. In this new world, I have observed that the political interest groups are remarkable not only for their variety but also for their specialization. I here record a random list of several that came to my attention in one recent session: the California Federation of Republican Women, Hikers to Free Our Parks, National Whistleblower Union, Citizens against Daylight Saving Time, Citizens for Finnish-American Power, the U.S. Committee to Support the Revolution in Peru, and the Anarchists Anti-Defamation League. If citizens communicate with the like-minded more than before, what their minds like is also more circumscribed than before.

In my own experience on the World Wide Web, I found that nearly half of the chat rooms and newsgroups reached through the most common gateways declare a preference for a particular point of view. The chat group designated as the second most popular on Lycos is "dedicated to discussion of politics from a right-wing perspective." Other sites, while eschewing commitment to partisans of left and right, nevertheless reinforce political cynicism: among those with the greatest "hits" is the homepage of Voters for None of the Above, a nonpartisan organization devoted to "giving voters the ballot option to reject all the candidates for an office."

I recognize that citizens may post on multiple sites and may take part in multiple organizations, just as they now join different, crosscutting interest groups (at least according to pluralist theories of contemporary politics). I also acknowledge that some users may occasionally log on to sites more out of curiosity than out of commitment. In general, however, it must be recognized that in the routine of surfing and posting on the Internet, citizens have both less need and less incentive to seek out sites and groups that embrace a broad range of interests and bring together a wide range of perspectives.

Furthermore, one should keep in mind that most of the activity on the Internet is not political at all. (This is the third factor that may impede factious combinations.) At the most popular gateways the categories that attract the most "hits" are entertainment, shopping, travel, people, and relationships.

These checks on the political potential of majorities perhaps should cause me, as Professor Dahl suggests, to be "enormously pleased." In some moods I confess I am. :-) The capacity of the Internet and its kindred technologies to reinforce the apolitical tendencies of citizens can help prevent politics from becoming excessively intense and politicians from suffering undue pressure. The less politically interested (and therefore less politically competent) devote their attention to other activities and leave government to those who know best.

Yet in a more reflective mood, I find that I am not so pleased. :-(Nothing is more important for good government than "fidelity to the object of government, which is the happiness of the people." To pursue this object, I would still rely on the people's representatives, who have at least more experience and perhaps more public spirit than ordinary citizens. However, these representatives are accountable to the electors—and more directly now than in my time. Representatives are likely in the future to be still more directly accountable as citizens take advantage of the populist potential of information technology. If most electors care little about politics, and those few who do care frequent chat rooms and newsgroups that cater only to their special interests, then representatives will stand at the mercy of electoral power that is at best indifferent and at worst inimical toward the public weal.

There are two ways of curing these mischiefs of the Internet: the one, by improving the citizenry; the other, by enlightening its representatives. The new technologies could assist in effecting both. Some Internet sites welcome diverse opinions from all citizens and set a tone that encourages participants to respect the views of others and to regard politics as an activity that promotes not only factional but also public interests. An exemplar is the Democracy Network, which promises interactive debates in which participants communicate with candidates for offices as well as with one another, drawing on the site's archives, which contain previous statements by the candidate and other information relevant to the campaign. The deliberative polls initiated by James Fishkin, which you cite, could also be made more effective by exploiting the virtues of the Internet.

Yet it is in vain to expect the new technologies alone to create sufficient public spirit on the part of citizens. In the first place, the Internet mostly reinforces the tendencies already present in the wider civil society. Left to their own devices, the providers will offer more advice on "relationships" than counsel on public policy. In the second place, even when citizens engage in political discussion in the proper deliberative spirit on the Internet, they may not become more public spirited. In Fishkin's deliberative polls, the participants usually changed their minds when they learned they were mistaken about facts but rarely when they confronted views that challenged their own values. In the third place, most citizens spend most of their time attending to their private affairs. Although familiarity with the business of private life may be of some assistance in governing, there is no substitute for the experience of carrying out the duties of public office itself.

It must be acknowledged that enlightened statesmen will not always be at the helm of the ship of state. We have no choice, however, but to rely on representatives, especially on the men (and women, I would now say) who are prepared to devote themselves to public service. It is this political class to which we should turn our attention, and it is this class for whom the new technologies may prove more effectual. I do not presume, as you evidently do, that our political leaders will use these new instruments to manipulate more than to instruct citizens in the pursuit of the public good.

Is there any reason to suppose that the new technologies can further this object? You mention their capability of providing plentiful quantities of information, which may be used for good or for ill. (I must say that I am thankful that the Anti-Federalists did not have access to so potent a medium during the ratification debates.)

Like other commentators, however, you ignore an important probable consequence of this superabundance of information. The greater the quantity and more variable the quality of information, the greater the demand for authorities who can assess its reliability and relevance. The fabrications and falsehoods to which the Internet gives voice may admittedly serve some useful purposes. As Matt Drudge has said, "All truths begin as hearsay." Even while half believing the rumors they find on the net, most citizens, I trust, will seek guidance about which ones they may fully believe, which stand some chance of becoming the political truths of tomorrow. The authority of the *New York Times* or the *Wall Street Journal* is no less, and indeed may be greater, in an era when its readers have access to the *Drudge Report*.

As in the good government I commend, so in the good technology I recommend, there will be a need "to refine and enlarge the public views by passing them through the medium of a chosen body of citizens, whose wisdom may best discern the true interest of the country." Although your paper neglects this need as a force in cyberdemocracy's marketplace of ideas, may I presume that you would agree that some leadership—some refinement and enlargement of public opinion—is not only desirable but also possible through the instruments of the new technologies? I am encouraged—by the declaration at the end of your paper in which you "root" for the "professional politicians"—to believe that you yourself would look not to the media barons but to the political classes to provide this species of leadership in cyberdemocracy.

You and I also seem to concur on the nature of deliberative democracy. Certainly I would aver that representative democracy is no less legitimate than direct democracy. Indeed, one of the great dangers of cyberdemocracy is that it can increase directness at the expense of deliberateness, exacerbating the imbalance from which our system already suffers. However, it is possible to agree with this conclusion, but for reasons quite different from those you and I affirm. You assess the balance between directness and deliberativeness according to how well it protects and promotes liberty; democracy for its own sake, deliberative or otherwise, is not the chief goal. In this I also concur.

However, you know, perhaps better than I, that some deliberative democrats—indeed, some who are your friends and colleagues—take a rather different view. You have courageously resisted their efforts to induce you to trade eighteenth-century tradition for twentieth-century innovation. ;-) The most dangerous theorists of this school, Professors Gutmann and Thompson, in their recent book, concede (or, I suppose they would say, insist upon) the value of representative democracy. They also make a point of defending liberty, which they believe a constitution should guarantee.

Yet while paying this apparent deference to liberty, they pose an insidious question: because citizens disagree about the meaning and implications of liberty, how can any individual or group justify imposing through the coercive power of the state his or her understanding of liberty on everyone else? Even the most thoughtful citizens and their representatives disagree about liberty; Mr. Jefferson and I did not always see eye-to-eye on such fundamental questions.

In my time, we were quite prepared to appeal to the authority of natural rights, but I doubt that you are, and certainly few of your fellow citizens would follow anyone who invoked such traditional notions. On what basis then should democrats decide what liberty means in practice? Professors Gutmann and Thompson, along with some other deliberative democrats, are thus led to say that citizens or their representatives should decide in a process of mutual justification that recognizes the equal moral standing of all citizens.

Although I would not go so far as to permit the meaning of liberty to be contingent on deliberation, I am more sympathetic to the aims of the deliberative democrats than to those of most of the other varieties of democrats who populate the intellectual landscape these days—the interest group pluralists, the game theorists, the postmodernists, the strict conservatives, and their ilk. Democracy should rest on more than voting, even votes for liberty, and should encompass more than bargaining, even bargains for the public good. All good democrats should welcome the deliberationists' call for sustained exposure to diverse opinions, recognition of the difference between reasonable and unreasonable disagreement, and openness to change in one's fundamental political views through interaction with one's fellow citizens.

It must be confessed that these worthy aims place a greater burden on the new technologies. If the Internet were asked to facilitate only voting, it would need not be interactive. If it were expected to provide for merely bargaining, it would need to be interactive only to the extent necessary for conducting negotiations. Democracy, properly understood, requires technologies that support forums accessible to citizens of diverse perspectives and opportunities for active and regular interchange, all governed by norms of mutual respect and openness.

In the spirit of those aspects of deliberative democracy that I can accept, and in the terms of those elements of cyberdiscourse I can apprehend, I propose five criteria for assessing the extent to which new technologies may promote the aims of democracy, properly understood. I shall not scruple to object if you conceive of them as the first five amendments to the constitution of cyberdemocracy (a bill of cyber rights).

1. Forums shall be open to all. (No bozo filters.)
2. Surfing shall be participatory. (No lurking.)
3. Interactions shall be sustained. (No churning.)
4. Posting shall be civil. (No flame bait.)
5. Downloading shall be transparent. (No cookies.)

These amendments will no doubt require interpretation, which will give some of your friends cause to reaffirm the need for more deliberation. Yet you and I know that, like all worthy liberties, these are best protected by statesmen who are able to discern the true interest of the nation. May these statesmen join, with more than deliberate speed, the ranks of the digerati.

4

WILLIAM A. GALSTON

The Impact of the Internet on Civic Life: An Early Assessment

SUPPOSE THAT IN THE summer of 1952 someone had convened a conference on the rise of television and the future of community. The symposiasts would have faced two crucial problems. First, social reality was moving faster than empirical scholarship. Television was diffusing at an explosive rate, from being a relative rarity in the late 1940s to near ubiquity only a decade later. In 1952 scholars studying the social effects of television might have noted, for example, how neighbors crowded into a living room to watch the only set on the block, and they might have drawn conclusions about the medium's community-reinforcing tendencies that would seem antique only a few years later.

The second difficulty would have been even harder to cope with. Reasoning by analogy from, for example, the automobile's effects on sexual morality in the 1920s, these scholars might have suspected that television's unintended consequences would turn out to be at least as significant as its directly contemplated purposes. They would have been hard pressed, however, to move much beyond this general insight to hypotheses with predictive power. The insertion of a powerful new communications medium into a complex social system was bound to reconfigure everything from intimate relations to the distribution of public power. But how, exactly?

According to Alan Ehrenhalt, the front stoop was one of the centers of social life in Chicago's blue-collar neighborhoods of the early 1950s.

During that decade, however, the penetration of television into nearly every home affected not only the dissemination of news and entertainment but also patterns of social interaction. Families spent more time clustered around the television set and less time talking with their neighbors on the street. The increased atomization of social life, in turn, had important ripple effects. Spontaneous neighborhood oversight and discipline of children became harder to maintain, and less densely populated streets opened the door for increased criminal activities.[1]

I do not mean to suggest (nor does Ehrenhalt) that television was solely responsible for these changes; the advent of air-conditioning also helped depopulate streets by making the indoors far more habitable during the dog days of summer. I do want to suggest that the present is for the Internet roughly what 1952 was for television, and that the methodological problems just sketched are the ones we face today.

In the face of such challenges, it is natural, perhaps inevitable, that our thought will prove less flexible and our imagination less capacious than the future we seek to capture. In our mind's eye, we may hold constant what will prove to be most mutable. One of my favorite examples of this (there are many) comes from an article published in the *St. Louis Globe Democrat* in 1888:

> The time is not far distant when we will have wagons driving around with casks and jars of stored electricity, just as we have milk and bread wagons at present. The arrangements will be of such a character that houses can be supplied with enough stored electricity to last twenty-four hours. All that the man with the cask will have to do will be to drive up to the back door, detach the cask left the day before, replace it with a new one, and then go to the next house and do likewise.[2]

As Carolyn Marvin points out, this vision of the future reflects the assumption of, and hope for, the continuation of the economically and morally self-sufficient household, unbeholden to outside forces, productively and privately going about its own business—a way of life undermined by the very patterns of distribution and concentration that electrical power helped foster.

I draw two lessons from this cautionary example. First, in speculating about the impact of the Internet on community life, we should be sensitive to the often surprising ways in which market forces can shape emerging technologies to upset entrenched social patterns. (This maxim is particularly important for an era such as ours in which the market is practically and ideologically ascendant.) Second, we should be as conscious as possible of the cultural assumptions and trends that shape the way we use, and respond to, new technologies such as the Internet. In this connection, I want to suggest that contemporary American society is structured by two principal cultural forces: the high value attached to individual choice and the longing for community.

Choice and Community

Scholars in a range of disciplines have traced the rise during the past generation of choice as a core value. Daniel Yankelovich suggests that what he calls the "affluence effect"—the psychology of prosperity that emerged as memories of the Depression faded—weakened traditional restraints: "People came to feel that questions of how to live and with whom to live were a matter of individual choice not to be governed by restrictive norms. As a nation, we came to experience the bonds to marriage, family, children, job, community, and country as constraints that were no longer necessary."[3]

In Alan Ehrenhalt's analysis, the new centrality of choice is a key explanation for the transformation of Chicago's neighborhoods since the 1950s. Lawrence Friedman argues that individual choice is the central norm around which the modern American legal system has been restructured. Alan Wolfe sees individual choice at the heart of the nonjudgmental tolerance that characterizes middle-class morality in contemporary America.[4]

The problem (emphasized by all these authors) is that as individual choice expands, the bonds linking us to others tend to weaken. To the extent that the desire for human connections is a permanent feature of the human condition, the expansion of choice was bound to trigger an acute sense of loss, now expressed as a longing for community.[5] (The remarkable public response to Robert Putnam's *Bowling Alone* can in part be attributed to this sentiment.) Few Americans are willing to surrender the expansive individual liberty they now enjoy, however, even in the name of stronger marriages, more stable neighborhoods, or fuller citizenship. This tension constitutes what many Americans experience as the central dilemma of our age: as Wolfe puts it, "how to be an autonomous person and tied together with others at the same time."[6]

I do not believe that this problem can ever be fully solved; to some extent, strong ties are bound to require compromises of autonomy, and vice versa. (This exemplifies Isaiah Berlin's pluralist account of our moral condition: the genuine goods of life are diverse and in tension with one another, so that no single good can be given pride of place without sacrificing others.) Still, there is an obvious motivation for reducing this tension as far as possible—that is, for finding ways of living that combine individual autonomy and strong social bonds.

This desire gives rise to a concept that I call voluntary community. This conception of social ties compatible with autonomy has three defining conditions: low barriers to entry, low barriers to exit, and interpersonal relations shaped by mutual adjustment rather than hierarchical authority or coercion. Part of the excitement surrounding the Internet is what some see as the possibility it offers of facilitating the formation of voluntary communities so understood. Others doubt that the kinds of social ties likely to develop on the Internet can be adequate substitutes, practically or emotionally, for the traditional ties they purport to replace.

Are Online Groups "Communities"?

Writing thirty years ago, J. C. R. Licklider and Robert Taylor suggested that "life will be happier for the online individual because the people with whom one interacts most strongly will be selected more by commonality of interests and goals than by accidents of proximity."[7] Whether Internet users are in fact happier—and, if so, whether they are happier because they are users—remains to be seen and may never be known (the problems of research design for that issue boggle the mind). The underlying hypothesis that "accidents of proximity" are on balance a source of unhappiness seems incomplete at best. Licklider and Taylor were certainly right, however, to predict that online communication would facilitate the growth of groups with shared interests. Indeed, participation in such groups is now the second most frequently interactive activity (behind e-mail) among online users.[8]

Anecdotal evidence suggests that these groups fill a range of significant needs for their participants. For some, the exchange of information and opinions about shared enthusiasms—rock groups or sports teams, for example—is satisfying as an end in itself. For others, this exchange serves important personal or professional goals. Those suffering from specific diseases can share information about promising doctors, therapies, and treatment centers more widely and rapidly than ever before. A friend of mine who works as the lone archivist in a city library system says that participating in the online group of archivists from around the country mitigates

the otherwise intense sense of personal and professional isolation. In this
sense, computer-mediated communication can be understood as raising to
a higher power the kinds of non-place-based relationships and associations
that have existed for centuries in industrialized societies.

But are these shared activities "communities"? What is at stake in this
question? One commentator skeptical of the claims of techno-communi-
tarian enthusiasm argues that

> a community is more than a bunch of people distributed in all 24
> time zones, sitting in their dens and pounding away on keyboards
> about the latest news in alt.Music.indigogirls. That's not a commu-
> nity; it's a fan club. Newsgroups, mailing lists, chat rooms–call them
> what you will, the Internet's virtual communities are not communi-
> ties in almost any sense of the word. A community is people who
> have greater things in common than a fascination with a narrowly
> defined topic.[9]

Note that this objection revolves around the substance of what members
of groups have in common, not the nature of the communication among
them. By this standard, stamp clubs meeting face-to-face would not qualify as communities. Conversely, Jews in the diaspora would constitute a
community, even if the majority never meet one another face-to-face,
because what they have in common is a sacred text and its competing interpretations as authoritative guides to the totality of temporal and spiritual
existence.

To assess these claims, we may begin with Thomas Bender's classic definition of community: "A community involves a limited number of people
in a somewhat restricted social space or network held together by shared
understandings and a sense of obligation. Relationships are close, often
intimate, and usually face to face. Individuals are bound together by affective or emotional ties rather than by a perception of individual self-interest.
There is a 'weness' in a community; one is a member."[10] Upper-middle-
class American professionals tend to dismiss this picture of community as
the idealization of a past that never was. Bender insists, however, that it
offers a tolerably accurate picture of town life in America before the twentieth century:

> The town was the most important container for the social lives of
> men and women, and community was found within it. The geo-

graphic place seems to have provided a supportive human surround that can be visualized in the image of concentric circles. The innermost ring encompassed kin, while the second represented friends who were treated as kin. Here was the core experience of community. Beyond these rings were two others: those with whom one dealt regularly and thus knew and, finally, those people who were recognized as members of the town but who were not necessarily known.[11]

Personal experience has convinced me that community, so understood, is not merely a part of a vanished past. On a trip to Portugal, my family stopped for the night at the small town of Condeixa, about ten miles south of the medieval university town of Coimbra. After dinner I went to the village square, where I spent one of the most remarkable evenings of my life. Children frolicked on playground equipment set up in the square. Parents occupied some of the benches positioned under symmetrical rows of trees; on others, old men sat and talked animatedly. At one point a group of middle-aged men, some carrying portfolios of papers, converged on the square and discussed what seemed to be some business or local matter. The square was ringed by modest cafés and restaurants, some catering to teenagers and young adults, others to parents and families. From time to time a squabble would break out among the children playing in the square; a parent would leave a café table, smooth over the conflict, and return to the adult conversation. As I was walking around the perimeter of the square, I heard some singing. Following the sound, I peered into the small Catholic church on the corner and discovered a young people's choir rehearsing for what a poster on the next block informed me was a forthcoming town festival in honor of St. Peter.

Many aspects of this experience struck me forcibly, particularly the sense of order, tranquility, and human connection based on years of mutual familiarity, stable social patterns, and shared experience. I was not surprised to learn subsequently that about half of all young people born in Portuguese small towns choose to remain there throughout their adult lives, a far higher percentage than for small-town youth in any other nation of western Europe.

Bender's examples of community (and my own) are place based, but it is important not to build place, or face-to-face relationships, into the definition of community. To do this would be to resolve by fiat, in the negative, the relationship between community and the Internet. Instead, I suggest that we focus on the four key structural features of community implied by Bender's account—namely, limited membership, shared norms, affective ties, and a sense of mutual obligation—and investigate, as empirical questions, their relation to computer-mediated communication.

Limited Membership

Although technical restrictions do exist and are sometimes employed, a typical feature of online groups is weak control over the admission of new participants. Anecdotal evidence suggests that many founding members of online groups experience the rapid influx of newer members as a loss of intimacy and dilution of the qualities that initially made their corner of cyberspace attractive. Some break away and start new groups in an effort to recapture the original experience.

Weak control over membership is not confined to electronic groups, of course. Up to the early 1840s, for example, Boston was conspicuous among American cities for the relative stability and homogeneity of its population, which contributed to what outside observers saw as the communitarian intimacy and solidarity of Boston society. Then, in the single year of 1847, more than 37,000 immigrants arrived in Boston, a city of fewer than 115,000 inhabitants. By the mid-1850s, more than one-third of its population was Irish. Boston was riven, with consequences that would persist for more than a century.[12]

Many kinds of groups can undergo rapid changes of membership, but they may respond differently. In a famous discussion, Albert Hirschman distinguishes between two kinds of responses to discontent within organizations. "Exit" is the act of shifting membership to new organizations that better meet our needs; "voice" is the ability to alter the character of the organizations to which we already belong. Exit is, broadly speaking, marketlike behavior, whereas voice is more nearly political.

I suggest a hypothesis: When barriers to leaving old groups and joining new ones are relatively low, exit will tend to be the preferred option; as these costs rise, the exercise of voice becomes more likely. Because it is a structural feature of most online groups that border crossings are cheap, exit will be the predominant response to dissatisfaction. If so, it is unlikely that online groups will serve as significant training grounds for the exercise of voice—a traditional function of Tocquevillian associations. In Boston, by contrast, because the perceived cost of exit was high, the Brahmins stayed put and struggled with the Irish for a hundred years, a tension that helped develop one of this country's richest political traditions.

In a diverse democratic society, politics requires the ability to deliberate, and to compromise, with individuals unlike oneself. When we find ourselves living cheek by jowl with neighbors with whom we differ but from whose propinquity we cannot easily escape, we have powerful incentives to develop modes of accommodation. On the other hand, the ready availability of exit tends to produce internally homogeneous groups that may not even talk with one another and that lack incentives to develop shared understandings across their differences. One of the great problems of contemporary American society and politics is the proliferation of narrow groups and the weakening of structures that create incentives for accommodation. It is hard to see how the multiplication of online groups will improve this situation.

Shared Norms

A different picture emerges when we turn our attention from intergroup communication to the internal life of online groups. Some case studies suggest that online groups can develop complex systems of internalized norms. These norms arise in response to three kinds of imperatives: promoting shared purposes, safeguarding the quality of group discussion, and managing scarce resources in what can be conceptualized as a virtual commons.[13]

As Elinor Ostrom has argued, the problem of regulating a commons for collective advantage can be solved through a wide range of institutional arrangements other than private property rights or coercive central authority.[14] Internet groups rely to an unusual degree on norms that evolve through iteration over time and are enforced through moral suasion and group disapproval of conspicuous violators. This suggests that despite the anarcho-libertarianism frequently attributed to Internet users, the medium is capable of promoting a kind of socialization and moral learning through mutual adjustment.

I know of no systematic research exploring these moral effects of group online activities and their consequences (if any) for offline social and political behavior. One obvious hypothesis is that to the extent that young online users come to regard the internal structure of their groups as models for offline social and political groups, they will be drawn to (or demand) more participatory organizations whose norms are enforced consensually and informally. If so, it would be important to determine the extent to which this structure reflects the special imperatives of organizations in which barriers to entrance and exit are low. The ideal of voluntary community reinforced by the Internet is likely to run up against the coercive requisites of majoritarian politics.

Affective Ties

Proponents of computer-mediated communication as the source of new communities focus on the development of affective ties among online group members. One of the gurus of virtual community, Howard Rheingold, asks whether telecommunication culture is "capable of becoming more than 'pseudocommunity,' where people lack the genuine personal commitments to one another that form the bedrock of genuine community."[15] He defines virtual communities as "social aggregations that emerge from the Net when enough people carry on public discussions long enough, with sufficient human feeling, to form webs of personal relationships."[16]

In this connection, the crucial empirical question is the relation between face-to-face communication (or its absence) and the development of affective ties. How important are visual and tonal cues? How important is it to have some way of comparing words and deeds? Here is one hypothesis: it is impossible to create ties of depth and significance between two individuals without each being able to assess the purposes and dispositions that underlie the other's verbal communications. Is the interlocutor sincere or duplicitous? Does he really care about me, or is he merely manipulating my desire for connection to achieve (unstated) purposes of his own? Does the overall persona an interlocutor presents to me seem genuine or constructed? We all rely on a range of nonverbal evidence to reduce (if never quite eliminate) our qualms about others' motivations and identities.

Internet enthusiasts respond to these questions by deconstructing the ideal of face-to-face communication. They point out (correctly) that duplicity and manipulation have been enduring facts of human history and the advent of computer-mediated communication raises at most questions of degree rather than kind.[17] I must confess that I come away unconvinced. Considerable evidence suggests that the Internet facilitates the invention of online personalities at odds with offline realities and that the ability to simulate identities is one of its most attractive features for many users (gender bending is said to be especially popular). However, the playful exercise of the imagination, whatever its intrinsic merits and charms, is not readily compatible with the development of meaningful affective ties. (Devotees of what might be called postmodern psychology, with its emphasis on social construction and bricolage and rejection of the distinction between surface and depth, might want to quarrel with this. So be it. I see no way of discussing affective ties without invoking some distinction between genuine and spurious emotions and identities.)

Another hotly debated issue is the relation between computer-mediated communication and the tendency to express strong sentiments in antisocial ways. Some researchers have argued that because the absence of visual and tonal cues makes it more difficult to see the pain words can inflict, the Internet reduces restraints on verbal behavior and invites individuals to communicate in impulsive ways. (An analogy would be the asserted desensitizing effects of high-altitude bombing.) Other researchers argue that it is precisely the absence of traditional cues that promotes the formation of social norms for Internet speech and that there is no evidence that this speech is more antisocial on average than is face-to-face communication.[18] Given the fragmentary evidence, I see no way of resolving this debate right now. Speaking anecdotally, the controversy and bitterness stirred up by comments on my synagogue's Listserv suggest to me that the pessimists may have the stronger case. Once an initial provocation occurs, the nature of the medium makes it easy to escalate the dispute in ways that might be muted in a face-to-face group. (In the interest of full disclosure, I should note that some members of my synagogue, on the basis of past controversies, believe that face-to-face exchanges on the disputed topics would have been equally uncivil.)

Mutual Obligation

The final dimension of community to be considered is the development of a sense of mutual obligation among members. Recall John Winthrop's famous depiction of the communal ideal aboard the *Arbella*: "We must entertain each other in brotherly affection, we must be willing to abridge ourselves of our superfluities, for the supply of others' necessities. We must delight in each other, make others' conditions our own, rejoice together, mourn together, labor and suffer together."[19] Winthrop's demands may be too stringent, but at the very least community requires some heightened identification with other members that engenders a willingness to sacrifice on their behalf.

The technology critic Neil Postman argues that whatever may be the case with norms and emotions, there is no evidence that participants in online groups develop a meaningful sense of reciprocal responsibility or mutual obligation. Groups formed out of common interests need not develop obligations because by definition the interest of each individual is served by participating in the group. (When that ceases to be the case, it is almost costless to leave the group.) The problem is that bonds created by interests (in either sense of the term) provide no basis for the surrender of interests—that is, for sacrifice.[20]

I find it intriguing that many defenders of online groups concede Postman's factual premise but deny its normative relevance. Nessim Watson, for example, argues that communities characterized by a strong sense of mutual obligation have virtually disappeared in contemporary America; to single out online groups for criticism on this score is both unfair and an exercise in nostalgia. Efforts to resuscitate the obsolescent idea of mutual obligation are likely to prove counterproductive: "Those who champion Postman's noble metaphor of community as common obligation are most often faced with the task of dragging other community members kicking and screaming into their part of the obligation. Attempts to construct community usually result in the increased frustration of organizers and the increased cynicism of participants toward the entire idea of community." In late-twentieth-century America, Watson concludes, there is no alternative to voluntary community based on perceptions of individual interest; we will have to get along as best we can without antique norms and practices of sacrifice and mutual obligation.[21]

I very much doubt that our society, or any society, can indefinitely do without these civic virtues.[22] The question of whether emerging forms of group activity help foster these virtues or reinforce their absence is likely to prove significant for the future. The magnitude of the impact will depend in part on the consequences of online activities for more traditional forms of group activity. I now turn to that question.

Online Groups and Place-Based Communities

In the 1996 Survey of Civic Involvement, the American Association of Retired Persons (AARP) explored current community understandings and practices (table 4-1). One of the survey questions asks respondents about their conceptions of community: "We often hear people talking about some community, or about things going on in their communities. If I were to ask you about 'your community,' what community would come to mind?" The organization's report on the survey notes that "up to three separate responses were permitted and recorded." Only 15 percent of respondents failed to offer any example of what they considered to be a community.[23]

It is clear from the survey results that for most people, community is still a territorial concept: 35 percent cited village, town, city, or county; 30 percent mentioned neighborhood, subdivision, or street. Overall, 59 percent of the entire sample offered one or more territorial examples of community. Formal organizations and voluntary associations (Tocquevillian America or, if you like, Putnamville) were cited by 34 percent of all respondents. Twenty-nine percent mentioned churches or faith-based organizations; no other type of association was mentioned by as many as 4 percent of respondents. Informal and "abstract" groupings and collectivities also came up frequently, with at least one example cited by 39 percent of all respondents. The authors of the survey note that although numerous respondents mentioned non-place-based examples of community, electronic information groups were conspicuous by their absence:

> Although the majority of respondents say they have used a computer in the past year, computer groups or people with whom they connect by computer were almost never mentioned directly by the respondents. Surely many of them are starting to use their computers and the Internet to communicate with others in their communities, whether geographically or socially defined; but they have not come to think of the computer network itself as a significant form of community in its own right.[24]

Young adults are significantly less likely to cite place-based and formal organizations than are other adults and significantly more likely to cite informal organizations. They are also somewhat more likely to feel distant from all forms of community.

Among the computer users in the sample, those who participated in computer-mediated communication (e-mail or chat groups) ranked significantly lower in community attachment than those who have not done so. This would appear to suggest that for some users, computer-mediated communication serves as a replacement for more traditional, local forms of attachment. On closer inspection, it becomes clear that this result is entirely a function of the fact that young adults are more frequent online users and less attached to localities.[25] The question for the future is whether this pattern will persist as today's cohort of young adults, who have postponed marriage and permanent employment far longer than did their parents and grandparents, enters into the kinds of personal and economic relationships that historically have been correlated with place-based ties.[26]

Table 4-1. *Type of Community Cited, by Age Group*
Percent

Type of community	18–30	31–49	50–70	71 and older
Place	47.6	63.6	65.0	56.1
Formal organizations	24.5	35.9	39.2	41.1
Informal organizations	54.3	36.2	34.3	23.9
None	18.4	14.3	12.8	17.1
(N = 1,500)				

Source: Data from Thomas M. Guterbock and John C. Fries, "Maintaining America's Social Fabric: The AARP Survey of Civic Involvement," University of Virginia, Center for Survey Research, 1997, p. 3.

The AARP survey defines an index of social involvement based on the level of self-reported activity in ten key activities. The average American scored 6.3, the index range being 0 to 19. Sixty-three percent of respondents had used a computer during the past year; they had an average score of 6.7 compared with 5.6 for nonusers. (There was no significant difference between those who used computers for some mode of computer-mediated communication and those who used them for noncommunicative activities such as word processing or solitary games.) After taking age, education, and income into account, the study finds that computer usage had a "[statistically] significant but small effect" on social involvement.[27]

In sum, the AARP survey suggests that online groups have not had a strong generalized effect on either the theory or practice of community in America. There is evidence, however, of shifts among young adults. If this proves to be a generational effect and not merely a life-cycle effect (the jury is still out), then some of the characteristics of online groups discussed earlier in this chapter could over time have a significant impact on American society.

Combining Place and Cyberspace

The discussion thus far has drawn a sharp distinction between place-based and virtual communities. It is possible to combine them (or at least to try) by constructing place-based local networks. The Association for Community Networking estimates that there are now approximately 150 electronic or civic networks.[28] The pioneers of community networking hoped that it would lead to denser connections among local participants and increased civic engagement. These hopes have been fulfilled only in part. In a recent survey, Lee Sproull and John Patterson report that many of the participants in projects designed to encourage community networking

> spend most of their time in placeless or remote activity, rather than in activity tied to the local community. . . . Even in the BEV [Blacksburgh, Virginia, Electronic Village] project, which supports a large number of local business and community web sites and local discussion groups, respondents report that the project is more helpful for placeless or remote activity (friends outside Blacksburgh, 84 percent; national interest groups, 54 percent) than for local activity (neighbors, 24 percent; local interest groups, 30 percent).[29]

In short, it has proved surprisingly difficult to enlist modern information technology in the service of place-based communities. Although some intensification of connections among local residents does occur, the dominant effect seems to be the turn away from place toward placeless groups. As we have seen, there are good reasons to believe that the weakening of place-based ties entails substantial social costs and risks. Placeless communities are more likely to be thin communities.

On the other hand, we should be careful not to leap to apocalyptic conclusions about the social effects of the Internet, for good or ill. A standard thesis among students of social capital is that group membership tends to increase trust, which in turn enhances the cooperative capacities of the larger society. In a careful multivariate analysis of recent survey data, Eric Uslaner casts doubt on these hopes. He finds that involvement in online communities neither builds nor destroys trust. We bring our prior selves, the sum of our socialization, to the Internet; we use it, but it does not transform us. More broadly, there is no smooth path leading from involvement in particular communities (whether based on common place or common interests) and the "generalized social trust"—the ability to cooperate with strangers and those unlike oneself that large modern societies require. Uslaner insists that we are not likely to become more trusting in people unlike ourselves by interacting, online or offline, with people like ourselves. Instead, he concludes, such trust "reflects an optimistic world view and a belief that others share your fundamental values."[30] The belief that others share our values is linked, in turn, to the sense that they are like us in the most important respects. If so, the increased ethnic heterogeneity of the

U.S. population stemming from historically high levels of immigration and the increased economic heterogeneity resulting from emerging patterns of income and wealth distribution may turn out to be more significant determinants of social attitudes than are changes in information technology.

Voluntary Community, Information, and Attitude Formation

I return now to what appears to me to be the central issue in evaluating the likely effect of the Internet on civic life. Many Americans today are looking for ways to reconcile powerful but often conflicting desires for autonomy and connection. The idea of voluntary community draws its appeal from that quest: if we are linked to others by choice rather than accident, if our interaction with them is shaped by mutual adjustment rather than hierarchical authority, and if we can set aside these bonds whenever they clash with our individual interests, then the lamb of connection can lie down with the lion of autonomy. Online groups are paradigmatic examples of voluntary community—whence the enthusiasm they have aroused in many quarters.

It is far too early to know what kinds of effects they will have over time on the relations between individuals and communities in America. However, four kinds of structural doubts can be raised about the civic consequences of voluntary communities: because they give pride of place to exit, they do not promote the development of voice; because they emphasize mutual adjustment, they do not acknowledge the need for authority; because they are brought together and held together by converging individual interests, they neither foster mutual obligation nor lay the basis for sacrifice; and because they bring together people who are alike rather than different in crucial respects, they may intensify current tendencies toward fragmentation and polarization in U.S. civic life. This final point may seem less than obvious than the others; let me expand on it.

To begin, voluntary communities tend to be homogeneous. When given a choice, most people tend to associate with others who are like themselves in the respects they regard as important. Above a relatively low threshold, most people experience deep difference as dissonant and unpleasant. Even when such differences need not be reconciled through explicit collective decisions, they suffuse the shared social space and reduce its appeal for many denizens. To be sure, many people experience differences of food, culture, and even opinion as stimulating, so long as they can sample them at will and leave when they choose. For most people, in short, diversity is a nice place to visit, but they do not really want to live there.

Because Internet communities are voluntary, they are more likely to be homogeneous than heterogeneous, and group homogeneity can have negative consequences. In an important theoretical paper, Marshall Van Alstyne and Erik Brynjolfsson show how the Internet can translate even weak preferences for those like oneself into the formation of homogeneous subgroups whose internal interactions far exceed cross-group communications, a condition they term "cyberbalkanization." Left unchecked, cyberbalkanization can yield results that are economically efficient (in the sense that no individual can be made subjectively better off by switching from more focused to less focused associations) but socially suboptimal. For example, the growth of hyperspecialized communities can slow the growth of scientific knowledge, which depends on exchanges of data and critical perspectives across group boundaries.[31]

In a related analysis, Bruce Bimber suggests that the Internet's probable effect will be the intensification of group-centered politics, a process he terms "accelerated pluralism." His argument rests on two empirical premises: first, that the Internet will not alter the fact that most people are highly selective in their attention to issues and information; and second, that the Internet lowers the costs of locating, organizing, and mobilizing communities of like-minded individuals. On the one hand, this development may be described as democratization of group politics, as reduced transaction costs increase the organizational opportunities of resource-poor individuals and groups. On the other hand, accelerated pluralism decreases political coherence and stability while intensifying fragmentation, as narrowly focused "issue publics" form for transitory purposes, exert single-interest pressure on the political system, and dissolve when their task is done. In the process, the power of more traditional public and voluntary sector institutions that enjoy some stability over time and work to integrate (or at least broker) diverse preferences is likely to erode.[32]

The rise of homogeneous communities tends not only to decrease intergroup community and increase political fragmentation but also to exacerbate the difficulty of reconciling diverse interests and worldviews. In a recently published book, Cass Sunstein summarizes a wide range of empirical studies, conducted in more than a dozen nations, that point toward a common conclusion: a group of like-minded people who engage in discussion among themselves are likely to adopt the more extreme rather than more moderate variants of the group's shared beliefs. It turns out that particularly high levels of polarization occur when group members meet anonymously, which is precisely what the Internet permits. By contrast, face-to-face discussion within heterogeneous groups is more likely to yield a moderation of views all around or at least an enhanced willingness to listen to evidence and arguments and to alter one's judgments.[33]

Conclusion

In today's cultural climate, the response to these doubts about the civic effects of voluntary communities is easy to anticipate: anything that restricts choice runs the risk of trapping individuals in webs of oppressive relations. What could be worse than that? My answer is this: Learning to make the best of circumstances one has not chosen is part of what it means to be a good citizen and a mature human being. We should not organize our lives around the fantasy that entrance and exit can always be cost free or that we can wall ourselves off from those who are different without paying a long-term social price. Online groups can fulfill important emotional and utilitarian needs, but they must not be taken as solutions for our current civic ills, let alone as comprehensive models of a better future.[34]

Notes

1. Alan Ehrenhalt, *The Lost City: Discovering the Forgotten Virtues of Community in the Chicago of the 1950s* (Basic Books, 1995), chaps. 4 and 12.

2. Quoted in Carolyn Marvin, *When Old Technologies Were New: Thinking about Communications in the Late Nineteenth Century* (Oxford University Press, 1988), p. 77.

3. Daniel Yankelovich, "How Changes in the Economy Are Reshaping American Values," in Henry J. Aaron, Thomas E. Mann, and Timothy Taylor, eds., *Values and Public Policy* (Brookings, 1994).

4. Ehrenhalt, *The Lost City*, chaps. 12 and 13; Lawrence Friedman, *The Republic of Choice: Law, Authority, and Culture* (Harvard University Press, 1990); Alan Wolfe, *One Nation, After All* (Viking, 1998). An influential formulation of this tension is found in Ralf Dahrendorf's *Life Chances: Approaches to Social and Political Theory* (London: Weidenfeld and Nicolson, 1979). Yankelovich ("How Changes in the Economy Are Reshaping American Values," p. 20) summarizes his argument thus: Dahrendorf sees all historic shifts in Western culture as efforts to balance choices and bonds. Choices enhance individualism and personal freedom; bonds strengthen social cohesiveness and stability. In societies in which the bonds that link people to one another and to institutions are rigid, the individual's freedom of choice is limited. As people struggle to enlarge their spheres of choice, the bonds that bind them together slacken.

5. A recent survey asked Americans in which decade in the past half century they would most like to have lived, given the choice. In every age cohort, the 1950s proved to be the most popular choice.

6. Wolfe, *One Nation, After All*, p. 132.

7. J. E. C. Licklider and Robert Taylor, quoted in Steven G. Jones, ed., *Virtual Culture: Identity and Communication in Cybersociety* (Thousand Oaks, Calif.: Sage Publications, 1977), p. 10.

8. "Technology and On-line Use Survey" (Pew Center for the People and the Press, 1996), cited in Pippa Norris, "Who Surfs? New Technology, Old Voters, and Virtual Democracy in America," in Elaine Ciulla Kamarck and Joseph S. Nye Jr., eds., *Democracy.com? Governance in a Networked World* (Hollis, N.H.: Hollis Publishing, 1999), p. 71.

9. J. Snyder, "Get Real," *Internet World*, vol. 7, no. 2 (1996), pp. 92–94.

10. Thomas Bender, *Community and Social Change in America* (Johns Hopkins University Press, 1982), pp. 7–8.

11. Ibid., p. 99.

12. See Doris Kearns Goodwin, *The Fitzgeralds and the Kennedys: An American Saga* (St. Martin's Press, 1987), chap. 3.

13. Margaret McLaughlin, Kerry K. Osborne, and Christine B. Smith, "Standards of Conduct on Usenet," and Nancy K. Baym, "The Emergence of Community in Computer-Mediated Community," both in Steven G. Jones, ed., *Cybersociety: Computer-Mediated Communication and Community* (Thousand Oaks, Calif.: Sage Publications, 1995); Nessim Watson, "Why We Argue about Virtual Community: A Case Study of the Phish.Net Fan Community," in Jones, *Virtual Culture*.

14. Elinor Ostrom, *Governing the Commons: The Evolution of Institutions for Collective Action* (Cambridge University Press, 1990).

15. Quoted in Jones, *Cybersociety*, p. 24.

16. Quoted in Jones, *Virtual Culture*, p. 121.

17. For a discussion along these lines, see Jones, *Cybersociety*, pp. 27–30.

18. For a summary and discussion, see Guiseppe Mantovani, *New Communication Environments: From Everyday to Virtual* (London: Taylor and Francis, 1996), pp. 98–101.

19. John Winthrop, "A Modell of Christian Charity" (1630), in Perry Miller and Thomas H. Johnson, eds., *The Puritans* (New York: American Book Company, 1938), p. 198.

20. See especially Neil Postman, *Technopoly: The Surrender of Culture to Technology* (Vintage, 1993).

21. Watson, "Why We Argue about Virtual Community."

22. For the reasons why, see William A. Galston, *Liberal Purposes: Goods, Virtues, and Diversity in the Liberal State* (Cambridge University Press, 1991), chap. 10.

23. Thomas M. Guterbock and John C. Fries, "Maintaining America's Social Fabric: The AARP Survey of Civic Involvement," University of Virginia, Center for Survey Research, 1997, pp. 29–30.

24. Ibid., pp. 31–32.

25. Ibid., pp. 44–45.

26. The AARP survey also finds that computer usage is positively correlated with organizational membership and that among computer users, those who participate in

computer-mediated communication on average join more offline groups than those who do not. In addition, computer users are more likely to engage in informal volunteer activities than are nonusers (ibid., pp. 63–64, 81). These results remain statistically significant after correcting for background variables such as income and education.

27. Ibid., p. 24.

28. Lee Sproull and John Patterson, "Computer Support for Local Communities," Stern School of Business, New York University, 2000, pp. 2–3.

29. Ibid., p. 3.

30. Eric Uslaner, "Trust, Civic Engagement, and the Internet," paper presented at the Joint Sessions of the European Consortium for Political Research, Workshop on Electronic Democracy, University of Grenoble, April 6–11, 2000, p. 6.

31. Marshall Van Alstyne and Erik Brynjolfsson, "Electronic Communities: Global Village or Cyberbalkans?" Sloan School, MIT, March 1997.

32. Bruce Bimber, "The Internet and Political Transformation: Populism, Community, and Accelerated Pluralism," *Polity*, vol. 31 (Fall 1998), pp. 133–60.

33. Cass Sunstein, *Republic.com* (Princeton University Press, 2001), chap. 3.

34. For related reflections on these themes and others, see Peter Levine, "The Internet and Civil Society," *Report from the Institute for Philosophy and Public Policy*, vol. 20 (Fall 2000), pp. 1–8.

5

PIPPA NORRIS

Revolution, What Revolution? The Internet and U.S. Elections, 1992–2000

THE MORE THAT Internet use expands, the more hyperbole and hot air arises concerning its possible consequences for public life. Similar hopes and fears about the power of technology to transform democracy accompanied the rise of other media like the wireless, talkies, and television. Systematic research has started to explore the impact of politics on the Internet for political parties, candidates, and election campaigns; for new social movements, interest groups, and organizational activism; and for the policymaking process and governing in an information age.[1] This study considers the potential consequences of the Internet for civic engagement—in particular, whether new technology will widen the pool of those who participate in politics or reinforce the existing participation gap between the engaged and the apathetic.

Mobilization and Reinforcement Theories

Interpretations about the potential for expanding political participation through the Internet differ sharply. On the one hand, mobilization theories claim that use of the net will facilitate and encourage new forms of political activism. Enthusiasts such as Nicholas Negroponte and Michael Dertouzos believe that virtual democracy promises a cornucopia of empowerment in a digital world. Edward Schwartz emphasizes the potential for a virtual community. Howard Rheingold argues that bulletin board systems are democratizing technologies used to exchange ideas, mobilize the public, and strengthen social capital. Lawrence Grossman anticipates the opportunities for shrinking the distance between governed and government using the new communication technology. Ian Budge argues that the World Wide Web will facilitate direct democracy.[2] The strongest claims of mobilization theories are that net activism represents a distinctive type of political participation that differs in significant ways from conventional activities such as working for political parties, organizing grassroots social movements, or lobbying elected officials. By sharply reducing the barriers to civic engagement, leveling some of the financial hurdles, and widening the opportunities for political debate, the dissemination of information, and group interaction, it is thought, the Internet will bring more people into active involvement in public life. For enthusiasts, the net promises to provide new forms of horizontal and vertical communication that facilitate and enrich deliberation in the public sphere.

In contrast, reinforcement theories suggest that use of the net will strengthen, but not radically transform, existing patterns of political participation. From this more skeptical perspective, the Internet will serve to reinforce, and perhaps even widen, the participation gap between the haves and the have-nots. Richard Owen and Diana Davis conclude that the Internet does provide new sources of information for the politically interested but that, given uneven levels of access, there are good grounds to be skeptical about its transformative potential for democratic participation. Graham Murdock and Peter Golding warn that the familiar socioeconomic biases that exist in nearly all conventional forms of political participation seem unlikely to disappear on the Internet, even if access gradually widens to reach the electronically disadvantaged. If so, the new medium may merely reproduce or even exacerbate the gap between the information rich and the information poor. Kevin Hill and John Hughes argue that because Internet activists are self-selecting, the Internet does not change people; it simply allows them to do the same things in a different way.[3]

One reason the Internet may reinforce existing patterns of participation is suggested by the "uses and gratifications" perspective in political communications.[4] This account stresses that, given varied media choices, Internet users have certain predispositions and needs that motivate them to seek different programs and sources: people going out for the evening, for example, may turn to Movielink.com, those interested in socializing can go to an America Online chat room, and those wanting international news may log on to the online BBC *World Service*. The primary functions served by the media are those such as information seeking, social companionship, and entertainment. This account may be particularly suitable for the Internet, where, far more than with television or newspapers, users actively exercise choice (clicking to another website, joining a different user group, e-mailing colleagues) and thereby control the communication process. This assumes that the choice of media sources is essentially purposive, fulfilling certain needs in the audience, rather than simply habitual (if we usually return to a few bookmarked sites) or incidental (if we surf at random).

There are therefore good reasons why both the mobilization and reinforcement theories may be plausible. It is difficult, amid the rhetoric and conjecture, to find systematic evidence that can throw light on this debate. Given the pace of change in communications, with use of the World Wide Web growing by leaps and bounds, we cannot hope to have conclusive answers about future developments. Much depends upon the political and economic conditions—for example, how far the public sector intervenes to level the playing field for access. Political activism on the net can also be expected to vary according to the electoral context—for example, levels of participation in low-key midterm elections and in presidential contests may be different. For all these reasons, we need to examine patterns of use evident in the 1996 elections and see whether they were maintained or changed in subsequent contests.

Analyzing Net Activism

This study analyzes patterns of net activism in the United States using evidence from the Pew Research Center for the People and the Press, which has carried out some of the richest surveys of Internet use based on oversampling of the user community. The June 1995 survey queried 997 online users, drawn from a representative telephone survey of the general population of 3,603. The October 1996 survey covered 1,003 online users. The November 1998 survey contained responses from 1,993 Internet users drawn from a representative telephone survey of 3,184 adults. We also use the May 1998 Pew survey of media consumption (N = 3,002) and the November 1998 postelection Pew survey (N = 1,005) to understand net activism in the midterm elections. Finally, this study draws on the Pew Center's survey of the Internet election news audience from October to

November 2000 (N = 7,426), including a subsample of online users (N =
2,876). These surveys posed questions about a wide range of media habits,
including use of old and new media, as well as about respondents' political
attitudes.

The comparison of use in successive campaigns allows us to compare
patterns in the different environments created by presidential and midterm
elections. These surveys allow us to explore four related issues. The first
issue concerns access and use: Is the Internet in the process of becoming a
new mass media? In particular, how rapid has been the expansion from
1995 to 2000 in Internet access and in political activism on the net? If
mobilization theories are correct, then political use on the net needs to
spread beyond an elite minority into the general population.

The second issue concerns whether the net provides alternative sources
of political information: If claims that the net will transform democracy are
correct, then online information should displace, not merely supplement,
use of traditional news media. The third issue concerns the social profile of
net activists: Early studies commonly found that, compared with the general population, net users were overrepresented among those with higher
education and income, among men, and among the younger generation.[5]
Support for mobilization theories could be found if the social differentials
evident in the mid-1990s have gradually closed as the user community has
expanded.

The last issue concerns the political profile of net activists: In particular,
compared with the electorate, are net activists distinctive in their civic attitudes, such as their levels of political trust, knowledge, and interest? Are
they different in their party preferences and policy attitudes? Answers to
these questions help us to understand whether net activism involves a distinctively new form of political participation, as mobilization theories suggest, or is merely "new wine in old bottles," as skeptics argue.

The Internet as a New Mass Media?

Mobilization theories assume that use of the Internet will expand so much
within the next decade that the size of its audience will eventually rival, and
perhaps even overtake, that for television and the printed press. The overall rate of growth in online activity has been phenomenal: the number of
Americans using online and Internet services has doubled every twelve
months for the past two years. Pew Center surveys have found that the
proportion of Americans who ever go online to access the Internet surged

from 14 percent in 1995 to 23 percent in July 1996, 36 percent in November 1997, 41 percent in November 1998, and 62 percent in November 2000. In addition, the Pew Center estimated that in May 2001 almost two-thirds of all Americans (64 percent) used a computer at home or at work, indicating the broader potential for access.

The extent of the shake-up in news habits caused by this development becomes apparent when we compare regular use of conventional and online media in the United States. Precise estimates about use of Internet news sources vary over time as the way people think about Internet "news" continues to change. Nevertheless, Pew Center surveys suggest that the percentage of Americans regularly getting news from the Internet (where "regularly" is defined as at least once a week) more than tripled over five years, rising from 11 million users in June 1995 to 38 million in November 2000. The most popular daily online activities, as recorded in the November 2000 Pew survey, were sending or reading e-mail (an activity performed by 49 percent), getting news online (22 percent), looking for information about a hobby or interest (19 percent), looking for news about politics and the campaign (17 percent), getting financial information (13 percent), and buying products online, such as books, music, toys, or clothing (5 percent). Therefore, although many dot-coms hoped that the Internet would become the mall of America, by the end of the presidential campaign three times as many people were browsing for election-related information as were shopping. Moreover, about one-sixth of all Americans who used the Internet were getting their political fix online on a daily basis.

Yet we should not exaggerate the extent to which Internet news has taken over from traditional sources. Figure 5-1 tracks changes in the source from which most Americans got most of their news about the presidential campaign in successive elections from 1992 to 2000. The figure illustrates the dramatic hemorrhage of viewers in recent years from network television news, which served as "the most important campaign news source" for more than one-half of all Americans in 1992 but for only about one-fifth in 2000. Local television news also suffered a slight erosion of its audience, but in contrast, reliance on cable television, including CNN, MSNBC, and Fox News, as a major source of campaign news increased to one-third of all voters. According to the Pew Center survey, these trends cut across all demographic and social categories, although the preference for cable over network news channels was particularly marked among the generation under thirty years of age and, interestingly, among strong partisans more than independents and "leaners" to the right or to the left.

Figure 5-1. *Main Sources of Campaign News, 1992–2000*

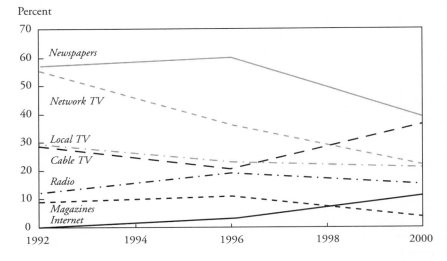

Source: Pew Research Center for the People and the Press, Survey (*N* = 8,378), October 10–November 26, 2000.
Note: The figure tracks responses to the question, "How did you get most of your news about the presidential election campaign? From television, newspapers, radio, magazines, or from the Internet?" (Accept two answers). If from TV, "Did you get most of your news about the presidential campaign from network TV news, local TV news, or from cable news networks such as CNN or MSNBC?"

The main reason for the decline of network news has been the fragmentation of cable and satellite stations and the balkanization of the television audience: the proportion nominating cable television news as their most important campaign news source rose sharply from 1996 to 2000. The reasons for the dispersion of the network audience to cable and satellite may well be mundane, as people may often find MSNBC or CNBC more convenient for their schedules than the NBC *Nightly News* at 6:30 in the evening. This phenomenon, however, combined with the growth of the Internet, has clearly caused greater competition for the major networks. The other winners from this process were radio news, which saw a modest boost in its audience, and news access through the Internet, which experienced a substantial increase. Overall only one in ten voters reported getting most of their news from the Internet, but almost one-third (30 percent) got at least some news about the campaign online.

How are we to evaluate these trends? In particular, is this shift toward digital technology as revolutionary as it appears? Not necessarily. According to surveys conducted by the Pew Center for their Internet and American Life Project during October and November 2000, most people usually surfed the mainstream news organizations, such as CNN.com (used at least once by 59 percent of online consumers of election news), MSNBC (used by 52 percent), the websites for broadcast TV networks (used by 45 percent), and the websites of national newspapers (used by 33 percent), rather than more specialized alternative outlets like *Salon* or *Slate* magazines (used by only 7 percent). Similar patterns are evident when Internet users were asked where they went most often for news about the 2000 elections: almost half of election news consumers (47 percent) said they frequented the websites of major news organizations such as CNN or the *New York Times*, and in contrast few often visited candidate websites (7 percent) or issue-oriented websites (4 percent). The Internet, then, appears to alter the mode and speed of transmission, and indeed patterns of revenue for the news industry, more than the use of trusted outlets. As with dot-com e-tailers, journalistic bricks-and-mortar sources with established reputations and credible authority seem more likely to survive and thrive in the information age than multiple upstart independents.

Why People Go Online

In America, in terms of the size of its total audience, the Internet can increasingly claim to be a mass media; this supports assertions of the transformative potential of this media. Is there a common experience of the net, so that we can talk about the effects of exposure to being online, much as we might discuss the influence of network news, violent movies, or talk radio? If so, then it is legitimate to generalize, as both sides of the debate often do, about the experience and attitudes of Internet users. Yet the fragmentation and segmentation of the World Wide Web, and the myriad of uses which the Internet can serve, means that perhaps we need a more cautious approach. Given the choices about where to go and what to do in the digital world, the question arises whether we have a shared experience of the web at all and therefore whether it constitutes a mass media in the conventional sense.

The need to refine our concepts of Internet users may be particularly important for types of net political activism. It is generally agreed that

political participation is not a single and uniform activity but rather a mul-
tidimensional phenomenon.[6] That is, people who regularly donate money
to campaigns or contact their congressional representatives are not necessarily involved in other dimensions like party work or community activism.
Different costs and benefits are associated with different types of participation. The main categories distinguished by Sidney Verba and his colleagues concern voting, campaign work, communal activity, and contact
specialists. In addition, a few citizens are active across all dimensions, while
some are involved in none.

Following this approach, participation in virtual democracy on the net
can be understood to involve many different types of activity. Someone
checking the web pages of the Christian Coalition or reading Time/CNN's
Allpolitics, for example, may be engaged in a different sort of activity than
someone discussing a sexual scandal involving the president or a member
of Congress in users groups or e-mailing colleagues about the time of a
community meeting. To explore the dimensions of net use in November
1998, the Pew Center surveys asked users about how often, if at all, they
engaged in a wide variety of activities, such as getting information about
movies, travel, or the Dow Jones, chatting with people in online forums,
and engaging in political discussion. People were asked about ten types of
activity (see appendix 5A for details of the survey questions), and the overall pattern can be mapped using factor analysis.

Factor analysis reveals two distinct dimensions or types of activity on
the Internet (see table 5-1). On the one hand, general users were most
interested in using the net for news about current events, entertainment-
related information about movies and hobbies, and financial information,
using e-mail, buying goods online, finding practical guidance about
health, and communicating through online discussion groups. Just as
many people turn mainly to the sports results, television listings, or stock
market reports in traditional newspapers, so people seek a wide range of
"news," usually apolitical, on the web. Although some of this activity may
bring people in touch with public affairs, as people click from one topic to
another, this process is more accidental than purposive. In contrast, political activists more often went online to engage in political discussions, to
contact officials or groups about an issue, or to get specific information
about the 1998 campaign. Therefore, net political activists who sought
political information or communication can be categorized as a distinct
group within the online user community, as in society.

Table 5-1. *Use of the Internet by General Users and Internet Political Activists, 1998*

Percent

Activity	General users	Political activists
Get news and information on current events, public issues, or politics	77	. . .
Get news	76	. . .
Get entertainment-related information, for example, on movies or hobbies	59	. . .
Get financial information, such as stock quotes	57	. . .
Send or receive e-mail	52	. . .
Purchase goods or services online	49	. . .
Get health or medical information	46	. . .
Communicate with others through online forums or discussion lists	39	. . .
Engage in online discussions about politics	. . .	85
Contact or e-mail groups or officials about political issues	. . .	82
Get information about the 1998 elections	. . .	55
Variance	26	17

Source: Pew Research Center for the People and the Press, *Technology and On-line Use Survey, 1998: Over-sample of On-line Users* (*N* = 1993), Fieldwork, November 1998.

Note: The model uses principal component factor analysis with varimax rotation, with Kaiser normalization suppressing coefficients below .35. See appendix 5A for questions asked.

Were the Internet political activists a small minority? We can compare the most common general types of net activity, defined as those that occurred at least once a week among online users, during the 1998 campaign. As indicated in table 5-2, the most popular general uses included e-mail (regularly used by almost three-quarters of online users) and work-related research (regularly used by almost half). Searching for information about politics and current events was the next most popular activity, used at least once a week by 38 percent. Yet more active forms of civic engagement were used by far fewer of those online in the 1998 campaign, including political discussion (used by 4 percent) and contacting officials or groups about politics (4 percent). The comparison of the 1996 and 1998 campaigns shows that the greatest increase in use has been in e-mailing

Table 5-2. *Frequency of Activities, All Online Users, 1996, 1998*
Percent

Activity	1996	1998
Send e-mail	64	72
Do research for work	48	47
Get news on current events, public issues, and politics	39	38
Get entertainment-related information, for example, movies or hobbies	30	35
Get financial information	23	28
Communicate through online forums, discussion lists, chat groups	23	22
Do research for school	22	14
Get information about the 1996 elections	12	10
Get travel information	10	12
Engage in online political discussions	4	4
Contact groups and officials about political issues	2	4

Source: Pew Research Center for the People and the Press, *Technology and On-line Use Survey, 1996: Over-sample of On-line Users* (*N* = 1,003), Fieldwork, October 1996; Pew Research Center, *Technology and On-line Use Survey, 1998* (*N* = 1,993), Fieldwork, November 1998.

Note: Columns give percentages of all users who went online at least once a week for the specified purpose.

and in obtaining entertainment-related and financial information. In contrast, the proportions engaged in the more political types of activity hardly changed. Wider access to the web seems to have expanded the audience for general interest subjects, such as information about the weather or movies, much more than the audience for political or international news.

What do we know about the minority (15 percent of all online users) who went online specifically to get information about the 1996 and 1998 elections? If we look more closely at the type of activities among this select group we find that the most popular activities included getting information about a candidate's voting record, participating in an online poll, sending e-mail supporting or opposing candidates, downloading election information, and providing information such as e-mail or mailing addresses (see table 5-3). In all cases, however, this activity involved no more than 5 percent of the total online community and therefore an even smaller proportion of the general electorate.

Table 5-3. *Online Election Activities, 1996, 1998, 2000*
Percent

Activity	1996	1998	2000
Participate in an online poll	34	26	35
Get information about a candidate's voting record	n.a.	30	33
Get or send e-mail supporting or opposing a candidate for office	n.a.	22	22
Get information about where and when to vote	n.a.	12	16
Participate in online discussions	31	13	8
Contribute money to a candidate through a website	n.a.	n.a.	5

Source: Pew Research Center, *Technology and On-line Use Survey, 1996* (*N* = 1,003), Fieldwork, October 1996; Pew Research Center, *Technology and On-line Use Survey, 1998* (*N* = 1,993), Fieldwork, November 1998.

Note: Columns give percentages of the sample who engaged in the specified activity. The sample consisted of those respondents who went online to get news or information about the 1998 elections (15 percent of the online user community).

n.a. Not available.

Clearly, use of the net will evolve further in subsequent elections. As was true for the early years of radio or television, access will gradually widen as familiarity increases, especially in the next decade. Different types of elections—such as the more exciting and open presidential race in 2000—have the potential to stimulate greater public engagement. Candidates may also develop new ways to communicate interactively through the web. The passive web page, from which people get vertical access to "top-down" information, much as they would from conventional political leaflets, is gradually being superceded by more active designs allowing horizontal communication among networks of citizens and "bottom-up" feedback into the political process.[7] Nevertheless, such interactivity seems likely to continue to appeal most to the small group of mobilized and interested activists rather than reaching citizens with lower levels of political efficacy and confidence. The proportion of Americans currently involved in any form of online election activity suggests the need for caution in making judgments about the transformative capacity of the web for democracy, at least in the short term. Online access and use has certainly expanded sharply in the past few years, but the proportion of net political activists remains relatively small.

Does Online Information Displace Traditional News Media?

The most common political use of the Internet is to seek out information from a myriad of sources; but the question remains whether this represents a distinctive activity, as proponents of cyberdemocracy suggest. If people commonly browse the web to consult political sources not available elsewhere, such as the candidate web pages, nonpartisan organizations like Project Vote Smart, and official sites like the White House web page, such activity could encourage more active citizenship. The unmediated quality of candidate and party information, and some attempts at interactivity, are also potentially different from messages that have been filtered by the press. Marion Just, Ann Creigler, and Montague Kern conclude that people typically browse several related sites on the Internet so that it has real potential for making a broader range of topics and more diverse sources of information available to citizens.[8] On the other hand, skeptics argue that many people are using the net to access conventional media sources, like the *New York Times, USA Today,* or *Newsweek*, through the Internet rather than the newsstand. Previous studies have found that people who gravitate toward the online media are also likely to monitor the traditional media, so that there is considerable overlap.[9] In this regard news is flowing through new channels, but it remains recognizably traditional journalism. This pattern alters *when* but not necessarily *what* we watch or read.

To examine whether online news sources displace or supplement traditional journalism, I used the Pew Center 1998 survey data to compare those who regularly use online and conventional news media. The correlation confirms that use of online news was weakly but significantly associated with use of newspaper and radio news ($r = .08$, $p > .01$; and $r = .07$, $p > .01$, respectively), but there is no significant association with use of television news. This pattern is even more evident among the smaller group of net activists, who proved most interested in learning about the campaign from any available news media. There is also some direct evidence about this issue. Among people who regularly get news online, a few (11 percent) said they were using other media sources less often, but this finding was more or less balanced by others (16 percent) who reported using other sources more often.

Additional evidence is available in table 5-4, which looks at where people seeking political news went on the web during the 1996 and 1998 campaigns. The most commonly visited sites were those for the old media—

Table 5-4. *Most Popular Websites for Political News, 1996, 1998, and 2000*
Percent

Website	1996	1998	2000
CNN.com	42	23	59
MSNBC.com	23	23	52
Network television website (CBS, NBC, ABC)	27	26	45
National newspaper website	38	23	33
Local community website	20	22	29
House, Senate, or White House website	n.a.	13	16
C-Span	25	12	15
PBS online	n.a.	9	10
Online magazines (for example, *Salon* or *Slate*)	n.a.	2	7

Source: Pew Research Center, *Technology and On-line Use Survey, 1996* (*N* = 1,003), Fieldwork, October 1996; Pew Research Center, *Technology and On-line Use Survey, 1998* (*N* = 1,993), Fieldwork, November 1998; Pew Research Center for the People and the Press, Survey (*N* = 8,378), October 10–November 26, 2000.

n.a. Not available.

Note: Columns give percentages of sample who had ever visited the specified site for political news. The sample consisted of those respondents who said they got political news online during the campaign. National newspaper sites included the *Washington Post*, the *New York Times*, and the *Los Angeles Times*.

national newspapers and network TV—and cable TV websites. Candidate and official government sites were slightly less popular, as were some of the nonprofit organization sites like Project Vote Smart or Policy.com. This pattern suggests that news is not necessarily a zero-sum game: hearing an item on CNN about the drug Viagra or President Clinton's relationship with the White House intern Monica Lewinsky can spark interest in going online to learn more about these stories, and vice versa. In the short term online news seems to supplement, rather than replace, the use of conventional channels. In the long term, however, given the attractions of the net for the younger generation, it remains unclear whether this pattern will be maintained in future decades or whether online sources will gradually come to replace older types of media production and distribution.

The Social Profile of Online News Users

As advocates of cyberdemocracy see it, the opportunities provided by the net will eventually lower the barriers to participation and widen access to those currently excluded from the policymaking process. The low costs of setting up a web page, for example, and free e-mail means that even a small organization with an imaginative and effective design can appear as professional on the net as much larger rivals. Unlike costly television ads, the use of web pages allows smaller parties like the Libertarians or the Greens to compete on a more or less level playing field with the Democrats or Republicans. Yet skeptics argue that the familiar socioeconomic disparities in political participation, evident throughout public life, are unlikely to disappear on the net.[10] In the 1996 election online users displayed a clear pattern in their education, income, gender, and age. Online users in general, and online political activists in particular, were more likely to be well educated, affluent, younger and male.[11] Yet have these social differentials gradually closed over time as the audience has widened?

Table 5-5 shows the social profile of those who went online for news about politics during the 1998 campaign compared with that of the general electorate. The general trend has been for gradual closure of gender differences in online use in recent years, as women are found in increasingly greater numbers among new users. Nevertheless, if we focus just on use of the net for political news, the results confirm a marked gender gap in 1998, a pattern that reflects the broader gender gap in conventional forms of civic engagement such as party membership and interest group activism.[12] The online gender gap is most marked among the older generation, but it also persists among those under the age of thirty, of whom young men are the most frequent online users.

There is also a significant generation gap among online news users, with the disparities particularly evident among those under the age of thirty and over the age of sixty. One remarkable feature of the results is the predominance of young people seeking news online, a group that is least likely to turn to traditional sources like newspapers. The May 1998 Pew survey found that among those in their twenties, more had been online the previous day (38 percent) than had read a newspaper (28 percent) or magazine (35 percent). In contrast, this pattern was reversed among the older groups. If this represents a generational shift in news habits, as seems plausible, then the gradual process of cohort change may eventually produce a major change in how people get their news, whether through inky linotype or over the wire. This provides some of the most important evidence in support of the mobilization thesis: online news and political information is now reaching the younger generation, who are currently least engaged in the political process and least attentive to conventional news media.

Table 5-5. *Social Profile of Internet Users of Online Elections News, 1998*

Category	Nonusers	Users	Statistical significance
All	90	10	
Gender			.31**
Men	44	60	
Women	56	40	
Race			
White	85	88	
Nonwhite	9	10	
Age			.37**
21–29	14	25	
31–39	22	24	
41–49	18	33	
51–59	15	12	
60 and older	31	7	
Income			.22**
More than $75,000	10	25	
$50,000–74,999	14	17	
$40,000–49,000	11	11	
$30,000–39,999	11	8	
$20,000–29,000	14	11	
Less than $20,000	15	5	
Education			.24**
College graduate	25	39	
Some college	27	28	
High school or less	48	32	
N	1,378	144	

Source: Pew Research Center for the People and the Press, Post-Election Survey, November 1998.
Note: Sample consists of those respondents who said they had gotten any news about the 1998 election from an online source. The coefficient of the association was measured by gamma.
**Significant at 0.01 percent.

    The disparities in terms of class and educational background confirm that online users remain atypical of the general public. In 1998 the most affluent (those with a household income of more than $75,000) were more than twice as likely to seek news online as their proportion in the total electorate. In contrast, the poorest groups and those with little education (those with a high school diploma and those who did not complete high school) remain strongly underrepresented among online news users. If we compare the background of online users in the 1996 and 1998 elections, the trends show income and educational disparities continuing, although they have closed slightly with the expansion of the online community. The familiar socioeconomic biases found in conventional forms of political participation, like voting, are therefore currently replicated in cyberdemocracy. The one exception to this usual pattern is found in terms of race: the evidence shows that minorities are represented proportionally in the news online community.

The Political Attitudes of New Activists

The mobilization thesis suggests that the new media will attract groups who might otherwise be uninvolved in conventional forms of activism, especially the younger generation, who have low levels of voter turnout and civic engagement, and those who feel alienated from mainstream society. In contrast, skeptics argue that "to them that hath shall be given": the people most likely to prove motivated to communicate and organize through the web are also those who probably would become most engaged in traditional forms of political activism in parties and groups and through lobbying efforts.[13]

According to table 5-6, which compares the political attitudes of all online users and Internet political activists in the 1998 election, net activists tended to be higher-than-average consumers of all types of media news, including television and radio. Net activists also displayed particularly high levels of reported voter turnout: not surprisingly, those who were most motivated to seek out news about the election were far more willing to vote than the average online user. This pattern is clearly reflected also in levels of political knowledge: when asked which party had control of the House of Representatives, net political activists were more likely than the average online user to get the answer right. There were no significant differences between net activists and general online users in levels of political and social trust.

Does use of online news have any impact on the outcome in terms of votes? In particular, what are the characteristics of net activists in terms of their partisanship? The patterns seen in the 1996 and 1998 data indicate that the group of net activists proved similar to the online community as a

Table 5-6. *The Political Profile of General Internet Users and Internet Political Activists, 1998*

Percent

Political activity	General users	Internet political activists	Statistical significance
Read paper yesterday	70	76	.15**
Watched TV yesterday	63	68	.11**
Listened to radio news yesterday	47	51	.09**
Voted in 1998	56	78	.46**
Voted Republican in 1998	42	44	n.a.
Voted Democrat in 1998	41	40	.04
Knew the GOP held House	62	80	.41**
Social trust: high	42	45	.04
Political trust: high	28	26	.02

Source: Pew Research Center, *Technology and On-line Use Survey, 1998*, November 1998.

n.a. Not available.

Note: "Internet political activists" are defined as those who engaged in online discussions about politics, contacted or e-mailed groups or officials about political issues, or went online for information about the 1998 elections. The coefficient of the association was measured by gamma.

**Significant at 0.01 percent.

whole in terms of their 1998 votes for representatives to the House. Nevertheless, there was a significant difference between the online community and the general electorate in terms of approval of House Republicans, online users proving more positive (see table 5-7). Moreover, the pro-Republican partisanship of online users was not simply the product of the gender, income, and educational biases among the user community, because approval of congressional Republicans remained a significant factor in predicting online news use even after controlling for the social background of voters.

Conclusions and Discussion

Voices can be heard claiming that for democracy, the Internet may produce the best of times or perhaps the worst of times. This chapter serves to confirm the overall pattern of reinforcement rather than mobilization: net political activists were already among the most motivated, informed, and

Table 5-7. *Political Predictors of Online Election News Users,*
November 1998

Variable	Coefficient	Standard error	R	Statistical sinificance
Gender	.90	.22	.14	.01
Age	.04	.00	.23	.01
Education	.15	.06	.07	.02
Income	.19	.05	.14	.01
Voted in 1998	.27	.22	.00	.24
Approval of congressional Republicans	.18	.08	.06	.02
Approval of President Bill Clinton	.01	.10	.00	.97
Constant	.55	.70		
−2 log likelihood	843.59			
Goodness of fit	1,316.07			
Nagelkerke R^2	.15			

Source: Pew Research Center, *Technology and On-line Use Survey, 1998,* November 1998.
Note: Logistic regression model, with use of online news in the 1998 election as the dependent variable.

interested in the electorate. In this sense, during recent political campaigns the net has been essentially preaching to the choir. The net still provided a valuable service in widening the range of information that was easily available during the campaign. However, the web has more often been used to access traditional news rather than as a radical new source of unmediated information and communication between citizens and their elected leaders. Whether the Internet has the capacity to reach beyond this group, and beyond these news sources, as access gradually ripples out to broader groups in the electorate remains an open question.

Sweeping generalizations about the positive or negative effects of the digital age are common, but they fail to establish whether there is one online community or perhaps many. Previous studies have often associated a single type of experience with going online. This chapter argues that we need to distinguish different dimensions of Internet use. What this study suggests is that, while we may hope for a virtual democracy, in which e-citizens become more politically engaged and informed, this activity may be confined to a minority. Some may choose to chat about political actors and the budget—or, more realistically, about the newest medical breakthrough and the latest doings of celebrities; this does not necessarily click the mouse of other types of users. Only a few members of the online community proved to be engaged in any form of political activity that can claim to be distinctively "new." Most online users are often using traditional journalistic outlets, like CNN or the *New York Times,* but from a more convenient source. Hence e-mails may gradually displace letters, web pages may displace reference books, electronic newspapers may displace inky linotype. Communication flows through new channels, true. But will this have major political consequences for patterns of participation? In the midst of this process of change, prognostications would be foolhardy. We need systematic longitudinal panel studies examining changes in media use, and any subsequent impact in civic attitudes, to explore this process further. There are persuasive grounds for skepticism, however, toward the more sweeping claims about the power of technology to change democracy as we know it. We all know that many tune out public affairs and tune in instead to MTV or the Home Shopping channel or the afternoon soaps. Given the fragmentation and choice of messages and activities available on the Internet, users may never encounter politics in their web bookmarks of choice. In this sense, although evolving into a mass media in terms of numbers, the net may never be a mass media in terms of a shared political experience. My Internet—where I go, what I read, what I do—is not your Internet. Such a customized media environment is empowering for users but also frustrating for analysts. In this sense, democracy.com looks more like anarchy than *ABC News.*

Appendix 5A: The Pew Research Center for the People and the Press, October 1998 Technology On-line Re-Interview: Factor Analysis Items and Coding for User Activities for Table 5-1

General Users

QUESTION 41: E-MAIL
Do you ever send or receive e-mail or electronic mail? If yes, ask how often:
1 Every day
2 Three to five days a week
3 One to two days a week
4 Once every few weeks
5 Less often
6 Never
7 Don't know

QUESTION 58: NEWS
How frequently do you go online to get news?
(Same coding as question 41.)

QUESTION 62: ONLINE ACTIVITIES
Please tell me how often, if ever, you engage in each of the following online activities:
62A: Communicate with other people through online forums, discussion lists
62B: Get financial information such as stock quotes or corporate information
62C: Do research for school
62D: Do research for work
62E: Get news and information on current events, public issues or politics
62F: Get travel information or services
62G: Get information about hobbies, movies, restaurants, or other
(Same coding as question 41.)

Net Political Activists

QUESTION 69: POLITICAL DISCUSSIONS

Do you ever engage in online discussions about politics? If yes, ask how often. (Same coding as question 41.)

QUESTION 70: CONTACT OFFICIALS

Do you ever contact or e-mail any groups, organizations or public officials about political issues or public policy questions? If yes, ask how often. (Same coding as question 41).

QUESTION 78: ELECTION NEWS

Have you gone or did you ever go online go get news and information about the 1998 elections? If yes, ask how often. (Same coding as question 41).

Notes

1. See, for example, Susan J. Douglas, *Inventing American Broadcasting, 1899–1922* (Johns Hopkins University Press, 1987); Iain McLean, *Democracy and New Technology* (Cambridge: Polity Press, 1989); Ian Budge, *The New Challenge of Direct Democracy* (Oxford: Polity Press, 1996); Wayne Rash Jr., *Politics on the Nets: Wiring the Political Process* (New York: W. H. Freeman, 1997); Christine Bellamy and John A. Taylor, *Governing in the Information Age* (Buckingham, Eng.: Open University Press, 1998); Kevin A. Hill and John E. Hughes, *Cyberpolitics: Citizen Activism in the Age of the Internet* (Lanham, Md.: Rowman and Littlefield, 1998); Richard Davis and Diana Owen, *New Media and American Politics* (Oxford University Press, 1998); W. Russell Neuman, "The Global Impact of New Technologies," in Doris Graber, Denis McQuail, and Pippa Norris, eds., *The Politics of News: The News of Politics* (Washington: Congressional Quarterly Press, 1998); chap. 6, this volume; Pippa Norris, *Digital Divide? Civic Engagement, Information Poverty, and the Internet Worldwide* (Cambridge University Press, 2001).

2. Nicholas Negroponte, *Being Digital* (Knopf, 1995); Michael Dertouzos, *What Will Be: How the New Information Marketplace Will Change Our Lives* (San Francisco: Harper, 1997); Edward Schwartz, *Netactivism: How Citizens Use the Internet* (Sebastopol, Calif.: Songline Studios, 1996); Howard Rheingold, *The Virtual Community: Homesteading on the Electronic Frontier* (Reading, Mass.: Addison-Wesley, 1993); Lawrence Grossman, *The Electronic Commonwealth* (Penguin, 1995); Budge, *The New Challenge of Direct Democracy.*

3. Richard Davis and Diana Owen, *New Media and American Politics* (Oxford University Press, 1998), p. 185; Graham Murdock and Peter Golding, "Information Poverty and Political Inequality: Citizenship in the Age of Privatised Communications," *Journal of Communication,* vol. 39 (Summer 1989), pp. 180–93; Hill and Hughes, *Cyberpolitics,* p. 44.

4. Alan Rubin, "Media Users and Effects," in Bryant Jennings and Dolf Zillman, eds., *Media Effects* (Hillsdale, N.J.: Lawrence Erlbaum, 1994); Denis McQuail, *Audience Analysis* (London: Sage Publications, 1997).

5. Davis and Owen, *New Media and American Politics,* p. 156.

6. Sidney Verba and Norman Nie, *Participation in America: Political Democracy and Social Equality* (New York: Harper and Row, 1972); Sidney Verba, Norman Nie, and Jae-on Kim, *Participation and Political Equality: A Seven-Nation Comparison* (Cambridge University Press, 1978); Sidney Verba, Kay Schlozman, and Henry E. Brady, *Voice and Equality* (Harvard University Press, 1996).

7. See chapter 6, this volume.

8. Marion Just, Ann Creigler, and Montague Kern, *Information, Persuasion, and Solidarity: Civic Uses of the Internet in Campaign '96,* paper presented at the annual meeting of the Western Political Science Association, Los Angeles, 1998.

9. Davis and Owen, *New Media and American Politics,* p. 142; Hill and Hughes, *Cyberpolitics,* p. 35.

10. Murdock and Golding, "Information Poverty and Political Inequality," pp. 180–93.

11. Davis and Owen, *New Media and American Politics*, p. 156; Hill and Hughes, *Cyberpolitics,* p. 29.

12. Janet A. Flammang, *Women's Political Voice: How Women Are Transforming the Practice and Study of Politics* (Temple University Press, 1977).

13. Hill and Hughes, *Cyberpolitics,* p. 43.

6

ELAINE CIULLA KAMARCK

Political Campaigning on the Internet: Business as Usual?

IN THE COLONIAL ERA, very few political offices were open to election. Yet for the few that were, prospective candidates were expected to personally meet every constituent and to offer them opportunities for food and drink—of the alcoholic variety. One contemporary referred to this as "swilling the planters with bumbo,"[1] a tradition that lives on in American electioneering in the form of oyster roasts, fish fries, and "rubber chicken" dinners. The fueling of voters with food, and especially liquor, lasted a long time in spite of efforts to outlaw the practice. In 1777 one of our esteemed Founding Fathers, James Madison, attempting to imbue the process with a bit of dignity, refused to serve liquor to the voters in one of his campaigns. He lost.

In attempting to assess the impact of the Internet on political campaigns it is worth remembering that, like swilling the planters with bumbo, once dominant modes of electioneering take a long time to die, and new modes of electioneering take a long time to gain dominance. Robert Dinkin's history of American political campaigning makes this point: "Old ways often would be employed along with the new until the former were shown to be obsolete."[2] It is therefore not surprising that the Internet has firmly established itself in the repertoire of modern American electioneering devices without diminishing the importance of television or radio or any of the other more traditional campaign technologies. Because of this its impact so far has been incremental, not revolutionary. This should not surprise the student of American electioneering: a quick look back in time shows us that evolution tends to be the norm.

In the early days of the Republic "stump speaking" emerged as the most popular mode of campaigning: candidates would literally stand on a tree stump to harangue the crowds at horse races, cockfights, and church meetings. In addition, the number of partisan newspapers increased dramatically as the first American political parties developed. Candidates let the partisan press engage in character assassination of their opponents while they themselves remained comfortably above the fray.

By the Jacksonian era, the electorate had expanded considerably—by 1825 most white men could vote—and this led to the need for a new, more energetic mode of electioneering. Politicians found themselves organizing huge extravaganzas such as parades, rallies, and barbecues and traveling long hours in an effort to reach the voters. The campaign rally, complete with red, white, and blue bunting and hours of speeches by local notables, survives intact today—albeit as a backdrop for the television cameras. As the century wore on these political extravaganzas took on a military aura. Political parties created uniformed "marching parties" such as the Republican's "Wide Awakes," and the torchlight parade was born. To this day, Chicago has a torchlight parade on the night before each election.

A more sedate form of electioneering emerged toward the end of the century as voter registration laws, a product of the Progressive Era, served to restrict the electorate, and a new, smaller, more highly educated group of voters were courted by politicians who spoke to them in tent meetings, seriously expounding on the issues of the day. Replace the tent with the television studio set up as a "town hall" meeting and the method is familiar—and it is with us still. During this period candidates and parties started to market themselves with buttons, pins, and symbols, and campaigning began to resemble merchandising. The campaign button of the beginning of the century turned into the "banner ad" on the Internet at the end of the century—both are forms of marketing.

When the phonograph was invented toward the end of the nineteenth century, William Jennings Bryan became the first presidential aspirant to have his words recorded. He was also the first presidential candidate to appear in a brief campaign movie, though in this instance, at least, being the first to use a new technology did not help win the election. So-called early adapters in the world of Internet campaigning have also met with mixed results on election day.

Radio was first used in the election of 1924, when Calvin Coolidge spoke over a hookup of twenty-six stations. Its campaign uses were immediately apparent, and by the election of 1928, both political parties were spending large amounts of money on radio promotion. Al Smith, the Democratic Party's nominee that year, was cursed with a scratchy radio voice, and so it was not until Franklin Roosevelt, whose voice was well suited to the new medium, arrived on the political scene that radio technology demonstrated its political power—both in his campaign and in his subsequent presidency. The election of 1924 saw, in addition to the use of the radio, the forerunner of the campaign commercial, as candidates made short movies about themselves to run in the movie theaters. The first campaign consultants, Clem Whitaker and Leone Baxter, hung out their shingle in 1933 in the Bay Area of California and went into the business of helping campaigns sell themselves.

Thus by the mid-twentieth century, candidates were using several generations of campaign techniques simultaneously, a feature of American political campaigns that would remain dominant for the rest of the century. They would ride the rails and appear repeatedly at the back of the train to deliver the "stump speech." (The term lives on in spite of the absence of the stump.) Large rallies were still held, as were parades in the big cities and barbecues and picnics in the South. The radio was used extensively, as were specially made movies about the candidates.

The year 1952 marked the introduction of a new campaign technology, one that would dominate presidential politics, especially, for the rest of the century—television. Dwight Eisenhower was probably the last presidential candidate to ride the rails. By the 1960s candidates traveled on airplanes, and the rallies, stump speeches, and other trappings of American electioneering became settings for the television pictures. Television made candidates' statements even shorter than radio had (although both had cut considerably into the hours of speeches common to campaigns a century earlier.) The famous Kennedy-Nixon debate of 1960 introduced yet another criterion into the election campaign. If radio placed a premium on the candidate's voice, television placed an even more important premium on the candidate's looks and ability to speak before the camera.

In spite of the fact that old campaign tactics never die, television dominated American presidential politics and other major races for the last four decades of the twentieth century. In presidential campaigns especially, all other political activities took place in the context of television and what would appear on the evening news. By the 1996 presidential election, which was the first election in which the Internet would play a part, television had gone through its own transformation with the introduction of cable television. Cable ended the dominance of the three television networks and forced campaigns that had mastered the art of controlling the "free media" to learn to operate in a multichannel environment.

The Internet as a campaign tool was born into this multichannel environment. The Republican primaries in 1996 saw insurgent candidate Patrick Buchanan use the Internet aggressively and well. Both major-party conventions in 1996 were covered on the Internet, as were both major-party presidential candidates. Most observers credit the Republican National Committee and the Dole-Kemp campaign with the most sophisticated website—although, to state the obvious, it was clearly not a decisive factor in the race.

In 1996 the Internet was still a novelty in American politics, an interesting but not an integral part of anyone's campaign strategy; in the larger races at least, television still dominated. The Internet may have been a factor in the close Senate race of Senator John Kerry (D-Mass.), and it may have figured in the close gubernatorial race of Christine Todd Whitman in 1997. In both instances the new campaign technology proved to be highly effective in the last-minute mobilization of voters.[3] In general, however, the Internet did not play a major role in the 1996 election cycle. Bruce Bimber, of the University of California at Santa Barbara, in his study of Internet usage in the 1996 elections, found that it was rarely used as a medium through which to contact voters. Phone calls, letters, and personal contact were all preferred both by the candidates' organizations and by interest groups.[4]

Nevertheless, as the Internet grew so did expectations for what it would do to political campaigning. As the 1998 midterm election cycle dawned, some candidates and their consultants expressed skepticism about this new medium. Jim Krog, who managed Florida governor Lawton Chiles's successful gubernatorial campaigns, said, "If I were running a campaign I would have one [a website]. But I would not put a lot of money into it because I don't know what it's worth."[5] Krog's comment is representative of many campaign professionals at the time and even today. Because uncertainty is rampant in political campaigns, it is difficult to know just exactly what contributes to victory. Therefore, as we have seen, candidates tend to layer new campaign techniques and technologies on top of old. In 1998 candidates layered the Internet on top of television, radio, direct mail, phone banks, and precinct captains—making the Internet an explicit part of their campaign strategy—and the same held true for the campaigns of 2000, only more so.

Yet as the 1998 elections approached, the Internet skeptics were countered by the Internet enthusiasts. Phil Noble, an Internet consultant, confidently predicted that 1998 would be the year in which a candidate won or lost on the basis of his or her use of the World Wide Web. Putting aside for a moment the difficult issues of causality, Noble can claim prescience for 1998: the victory of independent Minnesota governor Jesse Ventura is credited in large part to his innovative use of the net. Other Internet enthusiasts were not so lucky. Wendel Turner, a West Virginia lawyer, pinned his hopes of upsetting Representative Bob Wise in the primary on his use of the Internet—only to end up with a mere 6 percent of the vote. Doug Ross, a candidate for the Democratic gubernatorial nomination in Michigan, had a well-articulated Internet strategy and a good website with interactive features as part of his campaign. Nevertheless, he came in third in a three-way primary.

By the 2000 election cycle the Internet was firmly entrenched in the routines of American political campaigns—although skepticism about its role remained. One survey of political consultants and information technology professionals taken in March of 2000 has found that the majority rated the role of the Internet in the 2000 election cycle as "somewhat important"; but by a margin of nearly three to one, more consultants thought it was "not too important" than thought it was "very important."[6] Although the presidential candidates made extensive use of the Internet in their campaigns and in the long drawn-out recount process that followed, it is probably safe to say that the judgment rendered by the political consultants in the spring of the election cycle would have been the same in the fall. Nevertheless, Senator John McCain's unsuccessful bid for the Republican nomination and Ralph Nader's unsuccessful effort to attain third-party status provide for us interesting glimpses into the future of the new medium. Before we get to the difficult question of determining impact, however, it will be interesting to see just how campaigning on the Internet grew and changed in the short time between the mid-term elections of 1998 and the elections of 2000.

Campaigning on the Internet in 1998 and 2000

In the middle of the 1998 election cycle, I led a group of Harvard students in surveying every congressional and gubernatorial race on the Internet.

Table 6-1. *Major-Party Candidates with Campaign Websites,*
1998 and 2000

Race	Total number of candidates		Candidates with websites	
	1998	2000	1998	2000
Senate	68	65	49 (72%)	59 (91%)
House of Representatives	780	824	274 (35%)	542 (66%)
Governors	73	20	69 (95%)	19 (95%)[a]

Source: Data for 1998 originally published in "Campaigning on the Internet in the Elections of
1998," in *Democracy.com? Governance in a Networked World,* edited by Elaine C. Kamarck and Joseph
S. Nye Jr. (Hollis, N.H.: Hollis Publishing, 1999) pp. 99–123. Data for 2000 from www.netelec-
tion.org, a website devoted to the study of the Internet in politics and maintained by the Annenberg
Public Policy Center, University of Pennsylvania, 2000.

a. The only governor in 2000 who did not have a campaign website was the incumbent governor of
Vermont.

The purpose of the study was to find three important facts about this new
campaign technology—how often it was being used, by whom, and for
what purpose. In the 2000 election cycle, I was on leave and deeply
involved in a presidential campaign and therefore unable to replicate the
1998 study. However, the Annenberg Public Policy Center followed every
aspect of the Internet campaign in the year 2000 and collected much of the
same data that I had collected in 1998. These results can be found at
www.netelection.org. Thanks to the Netelection project we can compare
the evolution of Internet campaigning.

As table 6-1 indicates, by the year 2000 the Internet was firmly established in the repertoire of campaign technologies. Nearly every major party
candidate in the 2000 election cycle had a campaign website, and that is
especially true of candidates in statewide races for governor and U.S. senator. The major-party presidential candidates each had a website. Use of
the web for campaign purposes went up slightly in the races for the U.S.
Senate between 1998 and 2000 but went up dramatically in races for the
U.S. House of Representatives, nearly doubling in the two-year period.

Of course, one of the reasons that Internet usage in House campaigns is
so much lower than in other campaigns is that House races are often
uncontested or barely contested. By the middle of the 1990s all congressional offices had official websites, so incumbents who faced little or no
opposition probably did not feel the need to maintain a campaign website

Table 6-2. *Incumbent and Challenger Major-Party Candidates with Campaign Websites, 1998 and 2000*
Percent

	Incumbents		Challengers	
Race	1998	2000	1998	2000[a]
Senate	70	85	74	95
House of Representatives	19	53	52	77
Governors	84	83	100	100

Source: See table 6-1.
a. Includes contestants in open seats.

as well. Table 6-2 compares Internet usage by incumbent and challenger major-party candidates. Challengers in both 1998 and in 2000 were more likely than incumbents to campaign on the Internet. In statewide races, the differences are insignificant. However, in House races challengers were far more likely than incumbents to make the Internet a part of their campaign. This was especially true in 1998, when more than twice as many challengers had campaign websites as did incumbents. In 2000 the gap between incumbents and challengers remained, but many more incumbents were making the Internet a part of their campaigns.

If challengers feel that they have to try harder and thus are somewhat more likely to adopt a new technology, we should expect candidates in competitive races—whether incumbents or challengers—to rush to use the new technologies in hopes of achieving the necessary extra boost. According to the data presented in table 6-3, candidates in competitive races are most likely to use the Internet, but because Internet campaigning in statewide races is more or less universal, the differences between all races and competitive races are not very significant. As in 1998, all major-party candidates in competitive 2000 Senate races maintained websites; the big differences are to be found in House races. Whereas in 1998 slightly more than half of the candidates in competitive House races were online, by 2000 that number had increased to 95 percent. This indicates that the overall gap in Internet usage between House races compared with Senate and gubernatorial races may have more to do with the smaller number of competitive seats in the House as compared with the Senate and, in some years, the governorships.

Table 6-3. *Major-Party Candidates with Campaign Websites,*
All Races versus Competitive Races Only, 1998 and 2000
Percent

	All races		Competetive races	
Race	1998	2000	1998	2000
Senate	72	91	100	100
House of Representatives	35	66	57	95
Governors	95	83	96	. . . [a]

Source: See table 6-1.
a. There were no governors' races in 2000 that were classified by the Annenberg Center as toss-up races.

The previous comparisons deal with major-party candidates only, and yet for many web enthusiasts the political power of the Internet lies in its potential to inject new thinking into politics. Certainly the web offers the possibility of organizing apart from traditional party structures, and this fact alone should make the web an attractive place for minor-party candidates. Yet, as table 6-4 illustrates, third-party candidates in 1998 and in 2000 did not use the web as much as their counterparts in the major political parties. Although web usage increased for Senate and governor's races between 1998 and 2000, it was stagnant for House races—in contrast to the large increases in web usage among major-party House races.

Most of the minor-party candidates with websites are affiliated with the Reform Party, the Libertarian Party, or the Green Party, and their sites tend to be simple and basic. Some of the sites are thinly disguised advertisements for businesses. In 1998 Kat Gallant, a candidate for the Senate on the Libertarian ticket in Arizona, had a site that featured her beauty salon. At Kat Gallant's beauty salon, a man could get his hair cut by a woman wearing lingerie. Other than a bizarre and incomprehensible saga of her cross-country journey on horseback, which ended when the West Virginia authorities took her horses away, there was little of a political nature on this site. Mostly it featured Gallant and her hairdressers in skimpy clothes and sexy poses.

While it is obviously true that third-party candidates can get access to cyberspace more easily than to traditional media such as newspapers or television, it may not be true that they will be more successful in finding converts in cyberspace. Kevin A. Hill and John E. Hughes, using data from

Table 6-4. *Minor-Party and Independent Candidates with Campaign Websites, 1998 and 2000*

Race	Total number of minor-party candidates		Minor-party candidates with websites	
	1998	2000	1998	2000
Senate	72	52	24 (33%)	29 (55%)
House of Representatives	295	441	103 (34%)	154 (35%)
Governors	78	8	35 (44%)	4 (50%)

Source: See table 6-1.

the Pew Research Center for the People and the Press, have found that Internet activists are no more Republican or Democratic than the population at large. Faced with third-party candidates, however, they were more likely to stick with the major parties than voters in the population at large.[7]

Table 6-5 compares web usage among major- and minor-party candidates. With the sole exception of the 1998 congressional races, where Internet use among major-party and minor-party candidates was equally low, major-party candidates are much more likely to use the web than are minor-party candidates. The low cost of setting up a website and the ease of communication and therefore organization on the web makes this finding surprising and counterintuitive. Nevertheless, despite the indication, based on the aggregate data, that the web is not the home of insurgent politics that some people once thought it would become, the web has had its greatest impact with respect to candidates who were, in some way, insurgents.

The Electronic Brochure

In 1998 most Internet campaigns looked like and functioned as electronic brochures, and by the 2000 election cycle not much had changed. Writing about the 2000 cycle, Jonathan Karush notes that "most campaign websites are merely online venues for traditional campaign information—biographies, press releases, and upcoming events."[8] In 1998, 81 percent of the congressional and gubernatorial election websites offered biographical information about the candidates and information on issues. Netelection's coding for the year 2000 was slightly different but shows a similar tendency. Seventy-five percent of the websites offered campaign position

Table 6-5. *Major-Party and Minor-Party Candidates with Campaign Websites, 1998 and 2000*

Percent

	Major-party candidates		Minor-party candidates	
Race	1998	2000	1998	2000
Senate	72	91	33	55
House of Representatives	35	56	34	35
Governors	95	95	44	50

Source: See table 6-1.

papers, and 91 percent offered biographical information on the candidates. Actual campaign speeches were less popular. In 1998, 20 percent of the websites offered campaign speeches, and in 2000, 15 percent of the sites had campaign speeches. In addition, campaigns used their websites to provide news about the campaign. In 1998, 49 percent of the websites offered updated news in the form of press releases, reports, or photos from recent events. The Netelection study noted that 55 percent of the election websites in 2000 had press release archives available on their site.

In 2000, as in 1998, the Internet was used primarily as another form of mass media, another channel in a multichannel environment. For campaigns, the ability to put out information that is "unmediated" by the press is an attractive feature of the Internet, although it is unclear just how important a feature it is to winning. One of the most stable findings about Internet users is that they rely on traditional news sources (the *New York Times,* the *Washington Post,* CNN, and the like) in their electronic version.[9] One survey of Internet usage from the fall of 2000 finds that although the presidential campaigns were doing a good job attracting their own partisans to their sites, they were less successful in attracting the prized "undecided voters." Internet users tended to visit one site or the other but not both. For instance, in one week in August of 2000 the Bush site had 467,000 visitors and the Gore site had 350,000 visitors, but only 60,000 people visited both sites during the same period.[10]

The problem with the Internet in both 1998 and 2000 was that candidates were not very good at driving traffic to their sites. "Visitor acquisition," as some in the business call it, is a big problem for campaigns on the Internet, and until it is solved the Internet is unlikely to replace television or radio as the dominant campaign technology. One of the earliest candidates to try to base a campaign on the Internet was Doug Ross, the unsuccessful candidate for the Michigan Democratic Party's gubernatorial nomination in 1998. As Doug pointed out to me in a conversation reflecting on his experiences, voters are accustomed to politics coming "uninvited" through other mediums. Candidates knock on doors at dinnertime. Candidates' phone banks call voters in the evening, they send voters junk mail, they interrupt voters' favorite television shows or their drive-time radio listening with commercials. All of this activity is uninvited, and though it is often ignored, it does not usually turn off voters.

Yet "uninvited" activity on the Internet takes on an entirely different meaning, and the flow of "spam" angers many Internet users. In 1998 Steve Langford, a gubernatorial candidate in Georgia, made news when, having infuriated many voters by his attempts to gain their support over the Internet, he had to publicly apologize and promise to stop using the Internet for solicitation.[11] As Kathleen deLaski of America Online points out, the Internet has been "a pristine environment."[12] Because of this, candidates are still a long way from being able to waltz onto voters' computer screens as freely (and without fear of retribution) as they waltz onto voters' televisions or car radios.

In the 2000 election cycle candidates worked hard at driving voters to their sites. Senator John McCain, who earned high praise for his use of the Internet in his explosive but ultimately unsuccessful race for the Republican presidential nomination, engaged in one of the most aggressive and controversial strategies—"meta-jacking." Because the World Wide Web is so large, the HTML (hypertext markup language) is written to help people find what they want. The HTML usually contains several different descriptions of the website. Included in the HTML for John McCain's home page, in addition to the standard variations such as "John McCain for president" and "McCain 2000," were the words "Bush for president," "George Bush for president," "Bush 2000," "Dole for president," "Elizabeth Dole for president," and "Quayle 2000." According to Christopher Hunter, "sites engaging in meta-jacking are borrowing from the value of a competitor's brand name to attract traffic to their own site. This is the most likely motive behind John McCain's mention of George W. Bush in his meta-tag, a practice which raises some interesting legal and ethical questions."[13]

The legality of this practice is unclear. Hunter points out that companies have sued competitors for trademark infringement when they have been found to be secretly using brand names in metatags. It is unclear, however, whether a candidate's name is a "trademark"—this is a debate best left to the lawyers. The point for our purposes here is that candidates are working hard at the problem of "visitor acquisition." Just because it was not solved in the 2000 election cycle does not mean that it will not be solved in the future. Changing attitudes about "uninvited" e-mails on the part of voters may create a business in e-mail addresses that is as profitable as the mailing-list business has been for many years. Technical ingenuity in moving traffic from the web to the candidates may also help solve what has been one of the major stumbling blocks to the use of the Internet as a campaign technology.

Although the problems with driving traffic to candidates' websites have limited the impact of the Internet on voters—especially undecided voters—thus limiting its impact as a campaign tool, no such problems exist when it comes to the press. As far back as 1996, Wayne Rash Jr., in his study *Politics on the Nets,* found that "a growing proportion of information found in the traditional media stems directly from the Net." He points out that, with news media and television cutting back on costs and focusing on a bottom line, the Internet has become an easy way for voters to keep up with the candidates.[14] In my own experience in Albert Gore's presidential campaign, the Internet was often used to announce policy positions deemed "too wonky" for the candidate's speech itself. For instance, Vice President Al Gore's commencement speech at West Point was accompanied by a defense issue paper that was released on the Internet. Reporters were directed to the Internet as well as to the speech itself. Whatever the limits of the Internet for citizen information, it has become an invaluable source for the press. One survey reports that 93 percent of journalists go online for research and reporting.[15]

Finally, because candidates used the Internet primarily as a communication medium, they were careful to put their best foot forward. All campaigns with adequate resources conduct "opposition research." Most of it deals with the opponents' positions. Sometimes it deals with their personal lives, although most campaigns are quick to disavow any such investigations. Smart campaigns use negative research and negative attacks with care because such tactics have been known to backfire.[16]

Thus most of the material to be found on candidates' websites in 1998 and in 2000 was positive and upbeat. Usually even the name of the opponent could not be found on the candidate's site: "fewer than one in five active candidate websites reference the opposition candidate on the front page."[17] In 1998 only 22 percent of the websites contained negative or critical information about the candidate's opponent. Although the 1998 election took place against the backdrop of the explosive news of President Bill Clinton's affair with a young intern, only 3 percent of the websites in that election cycle criticized Clinton for the affair. In 2000, 30 percent of the sites contained what the Netelection people euphemistically called "comparative content."

When candidates did go negative, they tried to make the attack as entertaining or as factual as possible. For instance, the 1998 website for candidate, now governor, Jeb Bush of Florida offered a feature called "The Buddy McKay Tax of the Day." Also in 1998 the website of former representative Gary Franks, who challenged incumbent senator Chris Dodd, offered a feature called "The Top Ten Reasons Dodd Is a Hypocrite on Campaign Finance Reform." Comparative content in the 2000 races tended to be strictly on the issues. Elena Larsen and Steve Schneider cite examples of three congressional candidates in 2000 who made extensive comparisons on their website and note that they all tended to be heavily issue oriented.[18]

In the 2000 presidential race candidates were careful to tailor their negative comments to supporting the main lines of attack that had arisen in the debates. Sometimes they did this by creating separate websites. For instance, Bill Bradley's campaign put up a site called Moreaboutgore.com in which he detailed his claim that Gore was a conservative Democrat. Gore, in turn, put up a site (again separate from the main site but hyperlinked to it) called the "Bradley Information Bureau."[19] By the time the fall election was held, the Internet was used extensively to perpetuate the "spin" that emerged from the presidential debates. All in all, however, when negative comments appeared on the Internet they were muted and tended to hew to the issue differences. For the purists who bemoan the fact that the Internet is becoming one great shopping mall and losing some of its original "purity," the fact that the negative campaign—a staple of television, radio, direct mail, and phony phone banks—is so far a minor and muted part of Internet campaign strategies should be some cause for celebration.

Political Participation

There are several ways that interested citizens can participate in a political campaign beyond simply voting. They can make political contributions, volunteer, or engage in the much more informal activity of passing on political information to their friends. The Internet has made life for the campaign organizer much easier. As chapter 5 in this volume illustrates, however, there is not much data to support the thesis that the Internet has caused a revolution in political participation. A postelection survey of how citizens in the 2000 election used the Internet finds that the most common use of the Internet in politics was to send or receive e-mail jokes about the candidates or the campaign. Lagging far behind were such substantive activities as participating in a live chat or web-based forum (10 percent) and donating money to a political candidate (1 percent).[20]

Nonetheless, the low cost and immediacy of the Internet has made a difference in one of the most important tactical considerations of political campaigns—raising money when it is needed. In election year 2000 the single biggest Internet story dealt with fund-raising and was prompted by the large amount of money Senator John McCain was able to bring in following his upset victory over George W. Bush in the New Hampshire Republican primary.[21] As initially reported by John Mintz in the *Washington Post*, the McCain campaign "spent $300,000 on its Internet operations and . . . brought in $3.7 million through cyberspace, almost one fourth of its total $16 million raised." The average contribution to the McCain campaign on the Internet was $113, compared with the $30 average through direct mail, and 70 percent of McCain donors are first- or second-time political donors, with an average age of thirty-five.[22]

The power of Internet fund-raising is magnified in the presidential primary process, to which the Internet is a godsend. Unlike any other election in America, the race for the presidential nomination of a major party is a sequential affair in which candidates move from state to state in a series of primaries. The ability to score an early upset and then to turn that momentum into cash for later contests is crucial. The speed and simplicity of Internet fund-raising allowed John McCain the resources to contest subsequent key primaries in South Carolina and Michigan—making the use of the Internet a key strategic factor in his quest for the Republican nomination.

Although other presidential candidates took in money over the Internet, it was the insurgent candidates who raised the largest percentage of their money over the Internet. Insurgent candidate Bill Bradley's early success at Internet fund-raising and mobilization prompted the Federal Election Commission to rule that they would count donations made by credit cards as eligible for matching funds. (Previously they counted only money donated from contributors who signed checks.) This opened the door for

Internet fund-raising to become a major part of the presidential primary process, because the presidential primaries are the only elections in America in which candidates can receive a dollar in federal matching funds for every dollar raised (up to $250). McCain ended up raising one-quarter of his total over the Internet, and Bill Bradley, the challenger to the front-runner, Vice President Al Gore, ended up bringing in 6 percent of his money from the Internet. Al Gore and George Bush, favored by their respective party establishment from the beginning of the race, took in relatively small percentages of their money from the Internet—0.5 percent for Bush and 3.5 percent for Gore—although they raised much more money overall.[23]

There is no doubt that election year 2000 established Internet fund-raising as a key part of presidential primary fund-raising; all presidential aspirants had this capacity on their sites, and for the insurgents it was a conscious and integral part of their strategy. What about the other major races in election 2000? Unfortunately, it is not possible to compare Internet fund-raising in 1998 and 2000 because Netelection.org did not code for fund-raising, but we do have some evidence to suggest that raising money on the net in 2000 was probably as common as posting the candidate's biography. First, the intervening years saw the birth of several companies, such as eContributor.com, that sold easy and secure software to campaigns seeking to take online contributions. Second, one reporter, surveying the candidates in 1999, noted that "the possibility of raising significant sums through Websites at relatively little expense has politicians embracing the Internet with all the vigor and enthusiasm of '49ers staking a claim in a cyber gold rush."[24] Third, a review of candidates for the United States Senate has found that 98 percent of both Republican and Democratic candidates raised money on their websites.[25]

In 1998 fewer than half—42 percent—of the campaigns on the web provided information on how to make a donation, and only 11 percent went so far as to allow an interested person to make a donation with a credit card. Nearly half of all campaigns that year (47 percent) did not even bother to ask for money. Given that the "costs" of raising money over the Internet are virtually nothing (especially compared with the high costs of direct mail or chicken dinners), the failure in 1998 of more candidates to ask for money was surprising. Owing, no doubt, to this lack of solicitation, 1998 candidates raised relatively small amounts of money on the Internet.

The other way that citizens can participate in politics is by volunteering. In 1998, 50 percent of the election websites solicited volunteers for traditional campaign activities—including the sorts of activities that campaigns recruited for in the days before the Internet—manning phone banks and getting out the vote. Pat Buchanan's 1996 presidential primary campaign was probably the first campaign to recruit volunteers in cyberspace. By the end of the New Hampshire primary, he probably had gained more volunteers this way than anyone else.[26] In 2000 the two insurgent presidential candidates, Senator John McCain and former senator Bill Bradley, were also successful at soliciting volunteers over the Internet.

Just as political fund-raising on the web seems to have increased substantially between 1998 and 2000, it appears that soliciting volunteers increased as well. In the 2000 election cycle, 100 percent of Republican Senate candidates and 96 percent of Democratic Senate candidates recruited volunteers on their websites.[27] However, though volunteer activities on candidates' websites in 1998 consisted primarily of traditional (non-Internet) activities—such as driving voters to the polls and working telephone banks—in 2000 more and more campaigns, especially the presidential campaigns, were experimenting with "cybervolunteering."

Cybervolunteering seems to have appeared first in the 1997 gubernatorial campaign of Christie Todd Whitman in New Jersey and then reappeared in about 5 percent of the 1998 campaigns that maintained websites.[28] Cybervolunteering consists of a class of activities that can be done only on the Internet. The most popular cybervolunteer activity is a feature that allows a voter to send an electronic postcard to a friend—often with a personalized message attached. Another form of cybervolunteering is a variation on the old "visibility" campaign. Instead of putting a poster up in your store window you can put a "banner ad" on your home page. In 1998 Lily Eskelsen, a Democratic candidate in Utah, offered her supporters a "Cyber Yard Sign." In 2000 the presidential candidates, armed with greater resources and two more years' experience with the Internet, went even farther: Al Gore's website, for example, offered supporters the chance to build their own websites and create their own communities of Gore supporters—a tentative first step toward loosening the traditional campaign tendency to hold tight control over the campaign message. Cybervolunteering obviously takes more technical sophistication and more computer power than conventional forms of volunteering. For many House candidates, volunteering still meant signing up on the web for activities that were definitely not on the web.

The final and most important form of participation is, of course, voting. In 1998 only 11 percent of all campaign websites provided visitors with information on how to vote. By 2000 that number had increased to 23 percent of all websites—still not an overwhelming number. The modest amount of growth in the inclusion of what would seem to be such a simple and critical piece of information is consistent with a typical feature of election campaigns: a tendency to start out by putting time and attention into their Internet campaign and then to gradually forget about it as election day draws near. In 1998 fully 73 percent of the election websites online were not kept up to date and contained information that was more than a month old. Although we have no similar statistics for the 2000 elections, reporting indicated that a similar tendency was at work that year. Writing a few days before election day, Larsen and Schneider reported that "for the majority of candidate websites, the election is treated as though it is three months away, not three days from now. Political campaigns appear not to have figured out how to leverage the emotional intensity of the last few days of a campaign onto the Internet."[29]

Interactivity

The one feature of the World Wide Web that gives it superiority over television and radio, the dominant campaign technologies, is its capacity to be interactive. Yet there is surprisingly little interactivity on campaigns on the web, and candidates' rare attempts at interactivity have not gotten rave reviews. In 1998 only two sites, those of Tom Campbell, representative from California's Fifteenth District, and Tom Ridge, governor of Pennsylvania, had truly interactive sites. When I coded interactivity in the initial study, a site could be coded as fully interactive only if there was some ability to engage in a dialogue with the candidate or the campaign. Through a feature on his site called the Town Hall Meeting, Campbell invited voters to send him a message, to which he responded directly. Voters asked about campaign finance reform, about the budget, about cigarette taxes, about visa issues. Campbell stated that he tried to personally answer each message every day. Of course, there were only about ten questions a week. Nevertheless, the interaction was real, informal, authoritative, and linked to recent campaign events such as Campbell's appearance on a radio call-in show. There was none of the stilted prose that results when junior staffers use preapproved stock letters to respond to the mail.

The other candidate to experiment with interactivity in 1998, Governor Tom Ridge of Pennsylvania, invited visitors to his site to "talk with the candidates." This site handled the greater volume of inquiries that could be expected in a statewide race by scheduling online chat sessions among voters and asking them to sign a guest book in order to be scheduled to talk with the governor and the lieutenant governor.

In the 1998 study I had my researchers code sites as "fully interactive" only if there was evidence of some actual human interaction with the candidate. Many other sites in 1998 (72 percent) were, however, "partially interactive" in that they provided a forum in which the visitor could send an e-mail or answer a questionnaire. Other researchers have differentiated these two forms of interactivity by calling the first human-to-human interaction and the second media interaction.[30] Sometimes the partially interactive sites were nothing more than the web designers' nod to the new medium, without actual campaign endorsement. The home page of Jean Leising, Republican candidate for Congress in 1998 from Indiana's Ninth District, told voters that "Jean will occasionally share her personal thoughts" in response to the voters' inquiries—hardly a ringing endorsement of human-to-human communication.[31] In other words, on this dimension as on other dimensions of the Internet campaign the message appears to be "This campaign does not really have time for the Internet." Although the Netelection project did not code for full interactivity, we do know that a small number of candidates for the U.S. Senate in 2000 (4 percent of the incumbents and 9 percent of the nonincumbents) held interactive town halls, while nearly every one of the Senate candidates provided viewers the capacity to e-mail.[32]

The real barriers to true interactivity on the Internet are that it takes time and it threatens to divert the campaign from its message. Candidates do not like to spend time talking to people who cannot vote for them. In all but the presidential race, it is difficult to know where the voter is from, and thus a candidate could spend a great deal of time talking to people from another district, who will not be voting for or against him or her. The Internet may not have boundaries, but states and congressional districts do.

Second, control of the message in a campaign is as much an obsession as is money, and candidates fear this loss of control. In the 2000 election, the uncensored Listserv feature on Senate candidate Maria Cantwell's home page, in which comments about issues were e-mailed to the entire subscribed group, prompted the disapproval of many in the campaign.[33] In most interactive town halls, questions were screened by the candidate's staff, with the predictable result: the efforts were criticized as phony and the questions as "softballs."

John McCain held a widely publicized online fund-raiser during the primary campaign in which a live video feed featured the McCains at a table, with Cindy reading questions and John answering questions. Of the 250 questions submitted, John McCain answered twelve. The reviews from a web-savvy group of students who participated were not positive.[34] Other interactive attempts by the presidential candidates went largely unnoticed, and an Internet debate between Al Gore and George Bush garnered no attention and few viewers—especially when compared with the television debates.

In the few short years that scholars have been studying Internet campaigns, it has been assumed that the interactive potential of the Internet would be most important in the context of interactions between candidates and voters. Technology always has the power to surprise, however, and it did so in the 2000 election cycle. The most important interactivity on the web in 2000 did not take place in the context of candidate-to-voter dialogue but as an exercise in "strategic voting" or vote swapping, which took place among supporters of Ralph Nader and Al Gore.

The "Nader's Traders" websites that began appearing late in the fall presidential campaign created opportunities for Nader voters to "swap" votes with Gore voters in states that Gore was sure to win. The desire to trade votes is nothing new in American politics, but until the Internet, the capacity to do so did not exist. The 2000 election offered the perfect vote-trading incentives. Nader voters wanted to achieve the magic 5 percent of the popular vote, which would allow the Green Party to get federal matching funds in the next presidential election cycle. It did not matter to them where their votes came from, because they were not realistic competitors in the electoral college. Gore supporters, many of whom were sympathetic ideologically to the Nader voters, wanted to prevent Gore from losing votes in close states critical to the electoral college count in what was shaping up to be a very close election.

In this context the Internet offered the medium for a win-win situation—elect Al Gore president while establishing the Green Party as a party eligible for matching funds next time around. No wonder that the leading vote exchange site was called Winwincampaign.org. At its peak it was gathering about two hundred pledges an hour. The fact that the effort was ultimately not successful may have more to do with its late start than with anything else. Given the extraordinarily close electoral college vote and the excess of popular votes that Al Gore had in places like California and New

York, this exercise could have changed the outcome of the 2000 election and created an entirely new role for the Internet. The failure of Nader's Traders in 2000 does not mean that the effort is doomed. Given the winner-take-all nature of the electoral college, we can expect to see more sophisticated vote-trading sites arise in future presidential campaigns as voters, drawn to third parties of the right or left, seek to have their cake and eat it too.

Conclusion: Business as Usual?

In spite of the increased use of the Internet in the 2000 campaigns the Internet did not have that one clearly defined moment when it came into its own. Rather, it became another medium through which campaigns could conduct business as usual. The McCain campaign made fund-raising history on the Internet and established the strategic value of the net in presidential primaries once and for all. In spite of McCain's groundbreaking success at raising money, however, he still lost the Republican nomination. The traditional campaign of George W. Bush was simply too strong. Similarly, Nader's Traders showed the potential of the net for strategic voting in presidential elections, but this effort, too, was ultimately unsuccessful. The Green Party failed to achieve the threshold for federal money, and Al Gore failed to attain a clear electoral college victory.

Web enthusiasts are still waiting for the Internet to "make" a candidate in the same clear-cut, definitive way that television "made" John Kennedy in 1960. So far the nearest winner is Jesse, formerly "the Body" currently "the Mind," Ventura, a colorful former professional wrestler who stunned the political establishment by winning the Minnesota governorship on the Reform Party ticket in 1998. On November 6, 1998, Phil Noble, the Internet consultant, declared Ventura the "JFK of the Net"—the first candidate to successfully use the new medium.[35] As of this writing, Governor Ventura still holds that title.

Phil Madsen, the webmaster for the successful Ventura for Governor campaign, had a nuanced view of the influence of the Internet. At a conference following the election he observed that "the Internet did not win the election for us, but we could not have won without the Internet." In an example of just how hard it is to sort out the differing causal threads in a campaign, Madsen describes himself as a "website rookie" but a "skilled activist." In fact, the Ventura site was not one of the most elaborate websites in 1998—it lacked links to other sites, fancy graphics, and other typical website trappings. Its importance lay, rather, in the fact that unlike many of the sites in both 1998 and 2000, it was central to every strategic goal of the campaign. Its purpose, in Madsen's words, was to "produce volunteers, money, and votes."[36]

The Ventura campaign was, in fact, the first "virtual" political campaign. Until the very end, it did not have an office. When the campaign finally got an office it became a warehouse for the piles of T-shirts and other paraphernalia campaign workers were collecting to sell. By that time, this campaign was truly a "virtual" campaign—organizing everything from bus trips to finances over the Internet. Not only did the campaign raise about a third of its total dollars over the Internet; it also used the net to solicit people who would guarantee bank loans to the campaign.

Listening to this story prompted Robert Arean Jr., the former director of Internet strategy for the Dole-Kemp 1996 campaign, to comment that "if Phil had any candidate but Jesse 'the Hulk' Ventura, everything he did right would have been wrong."[37] That comment sums up what we have learned about this new medium thus far. It does not turn fringe candidates who are out of the mainstream and unattractive for reasons of message or person into winners. The Internet has not been a bonanza for extremist politics of any kind.

On the other hand, the major parties cannot rest easy. What the Ventura campaign and, to a lesser degree, the McCain campaign show is that the Internet can get an antiestablishment candidate much farther than would be expected. Overnight the Internet can compensate for years of fundraising and grassroots organizing if the campaign understands how to use it and if the candidate has something to say and appeals to voters.

As one of the first students of new media, Lawrence Grossman warned that "the only people more foolish than those who try to forecast the future of a new medium are those who listen to them."[38] With that in mind let me close with three thoughts about the significance of the Internet in campaigns to date. First, the Internet is likely to have its most spectacular impacts in the hands of insurgent candidates who "catch fire" for one reason or another. For these candidates who capture the imagination of the voters enough to draw them away from traditional candidates, the Internet can quickly make up for lack of party infrastructure. Second, candidates need to figure out how to drive traffic to their websites. Until they do so the Internet will be a useful tool for preaching to the choir but will not have the strategic ability to create winners and losers. Third, as the Internet generation ages and begins to vote, candidates will have to expand the interactive capacity of the web. Today's fifteen-year-olds will be eligible to vote in 2004, and they will have expectations of the web that are far more complex than those of their parents. As the first generation of truly multimedia voters they are unlikely to be tolerant of pseudointeractivity on the web, and their demands will drive the use of the new media.

Notes

1. Quoted in Robert J. Dinkin, *Campaigning in America: A History of Election Practices* (New York: Greenwood Press, 1989), p. ix.

2. Dinkin, *Campaigning in America,* p. ix.

3. See Marty Edlund, "Net Effects: How the Internet Changes the Costs and Benefits of Campaign Volunteering," master's thesis, Harvard University, 1998.

4. Bruce Bimber, "The Internet and Political Communication in the 1996 Election Season: Research Note," May 10, 1997 (www.wsscf.ucsb.edu/survey1/mobilize.htm [June 5, 2001]).

5. Quoted in Tim Nickens, "Internet, Candidates Click," *St. Petersburg (Florida) Times,* June 8, 1998.

6. The Democracy Online Project, Digital Democracy Databank, "Digital Snapshot," March 24, 2000 (democracyonline.org/databank/march 2000 survey [June 5, 2001]). The Democracy Online Project is a project of the George Washington University School of Political Management.

7. Kevin A. Hill and John E. Hughes, *Cyberpolitics: Citizen Activism in the Age of the Internet* (Lanham, Md.: Rowman and Littlefield, 1998), p. 36.

8. Jonathan Karush, "Cantwell Listserv," Liberty Concepts, June 11, 2001 (www.net-election.org/commentary/2000026.php3 [June 5, 2001]).

9. See chapter 5, this volume.

10. Jupiter Media Matrix, "Presidential Campaign Sites Capture Partisan Support but Fail to Reach Undecided Voters," October 18, 2000 (www.jup.com/company/pressrelease.jsp?doc=pr001018 [June 5, 2001]).

11. "Political News," *Wired News,* August 6, 1998 (www.wired.com/news/news/politics/story/13815.html [June 5, 2001]).

12. Kathleen deLaski, comments made at the John F. Kennedy School of Government conference, Politics on the Net: A Post-Mortem of the 1998 Elections, Harvard University, December 3, 1998.

13. Christopher D. Hunter, "Is John McCain Meta-Jacking?" (www.netelection.org/commentary/2000006.php3 [June 5, 2001]).

14. Wayne Rash Jr., *Politics on the Nets* (New York: W. H. Freeman, 1997), p. 118.

15. Ryan Thornburg, "Some Background Data on Online Politics," paper presented at the Democracy Online Project conference, What Is To Be Done?, Washington, January 21–22, 1999 (democracyonline.org [June 5, 2001]).

16. One famous example is Al Checchi, the millionaire California gubernatorial candidate who rapidly lost support in the polls after going negative against Jane Harman in the 1998 Democratic primary.

17. Elena Larsen and Steven M. Schneider, "Engaging the Opponent" (www.netelection.org/ commentary/2000034.php3 [June 11, 2001]).

18. Ibid.

19. Jennifer Stromer-Galley, "Candidate Websites Foster Debate, Not Negative Campaigning" (www.nelection.org/commentary/2000009.php3 [June 11, 2001]).

20. "Post-Election 2000 Survey on Internet Use for Civics and Politics," December 4, 2000, Democracy Online Project, Digital Democracy Databank (democracyonline.org/ databank/dec2000survey.shtml [June 5, 2001]).

21. See Jennifer Stromer-Galley and Steven M. Schneider, "The Logic of Internet Action" (www.netelection.org/commentary/200000/.php3 [June 5, 2001]).

22. Hugh Donahue, "News Coverage of the Internet and Politics" (www.netelection. org/commentary/200020.php3 [June 5, 2001]); John Mintz, "McCain Camp Enjoys a Big Net Advantage," *Washington Post,* February 9, 2000, p. A1.

23. Sonia Tita Puopolo, "The Internet and U.S. Senatorial Campaigns in 2000: An Analysis of Hillary Rodham Clinton's Website," master's thesis, Harvard University, 2001, p. 62.

24. Joan Lowy, "Grass-Roots Support Clicks; Politicians Jump on the Web with the Hope of Reaching More, Smaller Contributors," *Cleveland Plain Dealer,* August 1, 1999.

25. See Puopolo, "The Internet and U.S. Senatorial Campaigns in 2000," graph 8.

26. Rash, *Politics on the Nets,* p. 37.

27. Puopolo, "The Internet and U.S. Senatorial Campaigns in 2000," graph 8.

28. Edlund, "Net Effects: How the Internet Changes the Costs and Benefits of Campaign Volunteering."

29. Elena Larsen and Steve Schneider, "Ground Zero: The War without the Web" (www.netelection.org/commentary/20000037.php3 [June 5, 2001]).

30. See, for instance, Jennifer Stromer-Galley and Kirsten A. Foot, "Citizens, Campaigns, and Online Interactivity," paper presented at the annual conference of the Communication and Technology Division of the International Communication Association, Acapulco, Mexico, June 1–5, 2000.

31. Leising's website accessed at www.leising.org (September 30, 1998).

32. Puopolo, "The Internet and U.S. Senatorial Campaigns in 2000," graph 10.

33. Karush, "Cantwell Listserv," September 21, 2000 (www.netelection.org/commentary/2000026.php3 [June 5, 2001]).

34. See Kirsten Foot, "McCain's Cyber Express Webcast: Live and Interactive?" (www.netlection.org/commentary/2000008.php3 [June 5, 2001]).

35. Quoted in Rebecca Fairley Raney, "Former Wrestler's Campaign Got a Boost from the Internet" (www.nytimes.com/library/tech/98/11/cyber/articles/06campaign.html [October 28, 2001].

36. Phil Madsen, comments made at the John F. Kennedy School of Government conference, Politics on the Net: A Post-Mortem of the 1998 Elections, Harvard University, December 3, 1998.

37. Ibid.

38. Ibid.

7

DAVID C. KING

Catching Voters
in the Web

THE U.S. CONGRESS, the center of power and money in Washington and the brunt of countless jokes, has seen twenty-one decades of social and technological change in America. Now comes the Internet, still in its infancy, little more than a decade old. Is the Internet good for Congress? Will it fundamentally change the ways that politicians run for office?

If it is healthy for a democracy for its citizens to see, unmediated by the news industry, how public policy is made and how political coalitions are formed, then modern communication technologies are welcome. Public access to Congress improved tremendously with the emergence of C-SPAN television coverage in 1979 and through House Speaker Newt Gingrich's efforts to put House proceedings and documents on the Internet in 1995. The Senate followed suit, and today meaningful images of Congress are easily transmitted throughout the world. Because the Internet is asynchronous, it is easy to use in a democracy: not everyone has to be in the same room at the same time. In 2000 the civic site Freecomchannel.com, for example, made space on its server for candidates to upload ninety-second answers to any question—a capability that proved immensely popular.

The congressional galleries, balconies that ring the House and Senate chambers, are guarded and subdued, as they have been since the 1800s. Observers in the galleries may not take notes; pencils and pens can be confiscated; photographs are forbidden. Audience noises of approval or complaint can result in a closing of the galleries, as was accomplished by House Speaker Carl Albert in May 1972 while presiding over Vietnam War debates. Speaker Albert's reasoning was that the Congress could not deliberate in front of a mob without the threat of being ruled by the mob. The worry that an unfettered public may turn into a mob and diminish the quality of deliberation is still expressed on Capitol Hill. The World Wide Web has made it easier, though, to watch Congress at work. With television and Internet access, electronic galleries give citizens a better view of Congress than the physical galleries ever could.

The Internet in Congress

Today the institution of Congress uses the Internet as a tool for broadcasting proceedings and publishing documents. The websites House.gov and Senate.gov are gateways to Capitol Hill. Every congressional committee has a website, and historic documents are available through official websites of the House clerk and the Senate historian. Unlike public forums, however, along the Internet information from Congress flows in one direction, from the Capitol to remote users. Although almost every member of Congress has an e-mail address, e-mail messages are widely discounted by legislators as being less important than phone calls and postage mail, because e-mail is essentially costless to send. E-mail also has minimal impact because many lawmakers feel they are already inundated with information and opinions from nearly every social cranny.[1]

To the extent that Congress is a deliberative assembly that closely examines issues from various perspectives, the institutions that support deliberation tend to be deeply rooted in tradition. Committees hold hearings, as they have since the late 1700s, with witnesses carefully selected well in advance. Executive branch officials are routinely called to Congress, as they were in President George Washington's time. Interest groups from around the world send lobbyists to meet regularly with legislators and their staffs. Support agencies like the General Accounting Office, the Congressional Research Service, and the Congressional Budget Office provide valuable expertise.

Accurate and timely information is the currency that guarantees access on Capitol Hill. The Internet helps congressional staffers, lobbyists, and agency officials gather information for Congress, but legislators do not use the Internet for public debate and deliberation. Indeed, many legislators are loath to rely on web-based deliberations because they worry about bias on the Internet, given that web users are slightly more likely to be white and upper middle class. Many digital divides do exist, and one of the more interesting political imbalances is the presence of younger people on the Internet in far greater proportion than older people. Lawmakers are right to pay attention to digital divides and how they influence who contacts them online; but today's digital divides are less pronounced than the political ones that already exist. Fewer than one in five eligible citizens votes in congressional primaries, yet more than half of all Americans report having regular access to the Internet.

One should not expect Congress to become an Internet well of public dialogue anytime soon. To the extent that lawmakers continue to feel that too much information and too many opinions are already available to them, Congress will continue using the Internet as little more than a fancy all-hours viewing gallery in which citizens constitute the audience.

The Internet in Congressional Campaigns

Although Congress as an institution is unlikely to experience fundamental change because of the Internet, congressional campaigns will never be the same. The Internet makes it easier for campaigns to succeed at three critical tasks: marketing the candidate, knowing the voters, and getting voters to the polls. In campaigns, politics is marketing, and politicians can learn a lot about web marketing from General Motors and Nabisco. More important than displaying the product, marketers need to know who the consumers are likely to be, the preferences of their consumers, where the consumers are, and how to motivate the consumers to buy. How can the web do all this for political campaigns? There are time-tested ways of getting voters to the polls, and in a Darwinian way losing strategies (and candidates) are quickly discarded.

The keys to the future of the web in campaigns are evident in chapter 6 of this volume. These include the importance of competition to innovation, the use of the web to solicit campaign resources, the interactivity of the web, and the web's potential to knit together the internal organization of campaign staffs.

In 1998 congressional candidates used the web almost exclusively as an outlet for traditional campaign materials: press releases, appealing photos of the candidate, and basic contact information. These fit nicely into any traditional campaign, but the web coordinator of tomorrow's campaigns will be at the heart of any election strategy, and online resources such as PoliticsOnline.com and *Campaigns and Elections* magazine are poised to play a central role. The first campaign cycle in which the Internet is likely to sway voters in a sizable number of districts may be 2004, when Internet penetration is expected to exceed 75 percent of the population and a wealth of new voters, weaned on the web, will be coming to the polls.

In 2000 the web was widely used by congressional candidates for raising money, but the cluster of traditional advisers working on campaigns for Governor George Bush and Vice President Al Gore did not enthusiastically embrace the Internet. During the 2000 election cycle, the Republican Party raised nearly $250 million, yet just 2 percent of that was raised on the web. In six hours of presidential debates, neither leading candidate mentioned his website even once. The direct mail efforts of Republicans, who still preferred them as a fundraising strategy, were run by companies with years of experience in such campaigns. Untutored in web-based campaigns, the Republicans did not even ask respondents for their e-mail addresses, which compelled the nascent web campaign team to buy e-mail lists from the private market. Republicans had gathered 950,000 e-mail addresses by the end of the campaign, but more than half of those were acquired after August 2000, when partisans had already made up their minds on how to vote.

Candidates for Congress faired somewhat better using the web in 2000. In her study of Senate campaign websites, Sonia Puopolo finds near universal use of campaign websites as places to recruit volunteers in 2000. Every Republican candidate with a website recruited through the Internet, and all but one Democrat did, too. Similarly, all but one Republican and two Democratic candidates for the Senate raised campaign dollars on their websites.[2] In contrast, fewer than one in ten Senate candidates conducted "town hall" meetings through their websites, and barely one in ten used their sites to broadcast, in real time, campaign events. Successful and web-savvy campaigns of tomorrow will incorporate more webcasting and will deploy e-mail lists targeted at narrow slices of the electorate. As with product innovations in the private sector, web-based campaign innovations will emerge through the magic of political competition.

In his classic 1968 *Candidates for Office*, John Kingdon finds that winning candidates for Congress congratulated themselves upon making good strategic moves in a campaign (overestimating their own importance), and losing candidates rationalized their losses as the results of factors outside their control.³ This makes winning candidates (incumbents in the next election) more likely to follow strategies from previous campaigns, while challengers prove more likely to innovate and to take risks. It is through political competition that campaign innovations take hold, and these innovations are tested first by challengers.

Data on Internet innovations in political campaigns follow the Kingdon story closely. In 1998 Elaine Kamarck tracked the web presence (and absence) of 1,366 candidates (921 from the two major parties and 445 minor-party and independent candidates).⁴ Among Democratic and Republican candidates, web usage was twice as likely for challengers and contestants in open seats as for incumbents. Fifty-three percent of challengers and open-seat contestants had a website in 1998, whereas just 26 percent of incumbents adopted the new technology. In a similar study of congressional campaign sites in 2000, Steven Schneider finds websites to have been more prevalent among challengers and in competitive races, again demonstrating that competition spurs innovation in political markets.⁵

In the 2000 congressional campaigns, 52 percent of House incumbents and 85 percent of Senate incumbents had websites. Those are striking increases over the 1998 numbers, in which 19 percent of House and 70 percent of Senate incumbents had campaign sites. Incumbents learned about the power of the Internet through the proliferation of Congress-subsidized home pages, which were maintained by their own offices for communicating with constituents. In 1998 fewer than two dozen members of the House had office websites; by 2001 fewer than two dozen did not.

Some of the websites proliferating on Capitol Hill are surprisingly engaging. For example, Ohio representative Dennis J. Kucinich's official site boasts audio clips of polka music, including comedian Drew Carey singing "Too Fat Polka" and the great Frank Yankovic's "Beer Barrel Polka." Shortly after going online in 2000, the site was inundated by curious music fans and, presumably, occasional legislative inquiries. In a more sophisticated web maneuver just before Christmas 1999, Alabama Republican representative Bob Riley e-mailed constituents a video greeting, inviting them to visit his site and to respond to an online survey. Typical congressional surveys yield a 1 to 2 percent response rate; Riley's electronic outreach brought a 20 percent response in a district ranked near the bottom for Internet penetration. Representative Riley was the first, but by summer 2001, e-mailed greetings were in widespread use on Capitol Hill, proving far less expensive than bulk mail, although legislators continue sending mail in order to maximize the number of constituents they reach.

Capitol Hill may be the center of power in Washington, but it is easy to overstate and thereby misinterpret signals from the Hill. Legislators owe their existence to politically active clusters of voters "back home." The average member of the House of Representatives spends 172 days every year in his or her home state, and most lawmakers have developed personal and political networks specifically attuned to finding out what their voters are thinking. To this end, the Internet may be one of the best networks conceivable. Once this country had hundreds of local political machines. Machine politicos met immigrants in big cities, registered them to vote, helped them get jobs, and infused them with the spirit of American political culture. Politics was truly local, and voters were well known at the precinct level.

With the Internet, we hear the creaky beginnings of a new political machine. Like the organizing tools of yesteryear, the political Internet will narrowcast, focusing on individual interests and exploring block by block the virtual precincts of local issues. As members of Congress will quickly learn, the Internet can help political organizers communicate with finely drawn slices of the electorate.

For good or ill, the new political machine will bring us a new politics, too. The standard polka two-step (two hops to the right, two hops to the left) favors neither direction. It is the same with the new political Internet machine. Expect it to play all types of music and make lots of noise. With politics electronically linked to local interests, can that polka masterpiece, "Roll Out the Pork Barrel," be far behind?

Using the web, political organizers will identify and mobilize voters likely to support certain viewpoints without resorting to voter lists. Today, the e-mail addresses of candidates and interest groups are available to everyone in a congressional district.

Under current privacy laws, it is possible to buy the e-mail addresses of everyone who read a story in an online newspaper or used a web search engine to look for sites related to pollution. Who has gone online to read a review or buy a copy of *Girl Interrupted?* A mental health interest group may want to know. Indeed, a security breach in summer 2001 made available the e-mail addresses of about six hundred people who were using the antidepressant drug Prozac. Similarly, the e-mail address of a person who bought heart medication online recently will be a prized commodity the next time medical research funds are debated on Capitol Hill.

The upshot is a world in which interest groups, parties, and candidates can know what kinds of articles people read, what sites they search, what products they buy—all of that information linked to e-mail addresses. Do such fine-grained tracings of activity on the web exist? Some do, and the technology is here to build much more sophisticated profiles. It is simply a question of acquiring and merging electronic lists. Some of these lists are explicitly political, such as the information that thousands of users voluntarily provided to the now defunct Voter.com in 2000. That information was put up for sale in 2001, although most of the users were already politically active and engaged. What is more intriguing, highly effective political profiles can be drawn from information about consumer preferences. From a list of fifty movie titles, pick your five favorites. With that information, today's political analysts can make good predictions about whether you will vote and what characteristics you would like to see in a candidate. Interest groups would love that kind of information, because *Top Gun* fans are of a certain ilk, and *Othello* fans are another type altogether.

If all of this sounds frightening, perhaps it should, but to date Americans have shown little reluctance to give information on their buying patterns to supermarkets and video stores. Discount cards for purchases at supermarkets have proliferated, replacing coupons for most Americans, and buying habits are, where possible, linked to e-mail addresses that can be bought and sold. It appears that we want our preferences known, acknowledged, and accounted for. This may not be a bad thing. For example, online bookstores routinely make recommendations based on past reading patterns, and the majority of consumers say that they appreciate the suggestions, which build customer loyalty. Can campaign websites be tailored to the interests of voters in similar ways?

Use of the web in campaigns of the future will employ techniques that monitor voter preferences, mobilize selected voters around local issues, and build brand loyalty for elected representatives. Such loyalty used to be engendered with distinctly low-tech approaches when political parties were organized block by block and politicians regularly knocked on doors. As legislative districts have grown dramatically, doubling in size over the past sixty years, and as neighbors have become increasingly disconnected from one another, the web may be used to facilitate political communities once again.

Doug Bailey, dean of Washington pundits and the founder of the political newsletter *Hotline,* argues that the Internet

> can reestablish personal contact, which is what successful campaigns are really all about. Young people today, 11 to 16 year olds, live this way. They live on the Internet. And if the parties are to get young folks

involved, they will have to reach them through the Internet. That is the voting group that will dominate the politics of the future. This is a generation . . . that is going to change our politics in fundamental ways.[6]

Bailey's strategy is to move from high-tech to high-touch, with campaigns mobilizing not only their usual supporters but a cadre of web-savvy young politicos, as well.

As an example for ways that a web-savvy campaign might use the Internet, consider how we might have run a campaign for my friend (and noncandidate) David Hart.

David Hart for Congress

Mike Capuano won the 1998 Democratic primary in the Eighth District after Joe Kennedy (D-Mass.) retired. This being Massachusetts, the Democratic nominee was likely to capture the general election with only nominal Republican opposition, so the primary proved critical. Capuano had a website (as did his fellow challengers in the primary) that almost perfectly matched Kamarck's description of the 1998 offerings. It was little more than an electronic brochure. Much of the information was out of date, and though the site solicited volunteers, those solicitations were in no way targeted to specific kinds of voters.

Imagine that it is May 1998 and David Hart, a liberal Democrat in his late thirties, decides to enter the crowded primary, jumping in as the eleventh candidate. With such a crowded field, we can expect that just 20 percent of the primary vote could win the Democratic Party's nomination, but Hart faces four especially tough opponents: Ray Flynn (the former Boston mayor who has great grassroots "get-out-the-vote" skills), Marjorie Clapprood (who is well known as a radio personality), Chris Gabrielli (who has money to burn on television and radio but no neighborhood operations), and Mike Capuano (the wildly successful Somerville mayor who is not known outside of his town). Hart needs to identify and mobilize a niche of the Democratic Party that has not already been successfully targeted by his ten opponents. The web can help.

Identifying Likely Voters

Anyone who has worked in a campaign remembers purging and "scoring" voter lists. It is a monotonous process, but identifying quickly the subset of constituents who are likely to vote in the primaries is crucial to success. Nationwide, congressional primaries averaged just 17.4 percent voter turn-out in 1998, and candidates are careful not to "waste" time and money on the overwhelming majority of unlikely voters. Seeing who has voted in the past identifies likely voters, so every candidate in the Eighth District is work-ing from virtually identical lists. With the web, David Hart can do better.

Hart can begin by contacting the major web search engines (Google, Yahoo, Lycos, Excite, and Infoseek) and purchasing information about cit-izens whose zip codes locate them within the Eighth District. In early 1998 these search engines began offering free e-mail as a way of enticing users to yield their home addresses. (In 1997 identifying home addresses through web traffic was very difficult. No longer.) Hart can purchase, for example, the names, postal addresses, and e-mail addresses of every "web-registered" citizen in the Eighth District who has recently searched for "Ray Flynn" or "Marjorie Clapprood" on the web. For a small fee, a web portal (or search engine) can identify registered users who visited virtually any political web-site in the world, including very narrowly defined interests. If Hart wants to target, for instance, environmentalist voters, he can identify Eighth District web users who have searched for "the Sierra Club," "Ducks Unlimited," and so on.

Second, Hart should contract with Townonline.com, the online service of Community Newspapers—which has local papers in the Massachusetts towns of Watertown, Belmont, Cambridge, Brookline, and Boston. Online readers are encouraged to sign the site's guest book. This allows Townonline.com to identify specific users—and their usage patterns—any-time they reenter the site. A user registers once and is automatically iden-tified in subsequent visits. For a small fee, David Hart can buy the names, postal addresses, and e-mail addresses of every Townonline visitor who has read any particular story. Does Hart want to do a targeted Belmont mail-ing about the incinerator controversy? Then he needs simply to identify who has been reading about the incinerator online. This may be a little dis-concerting to people who care about their privacy, but anyone who is a reg-istered Internet user has almost no privacy. I registered to read the Associated Press Online through the *Los Angeles Times*. In theory, someone at the *LA Times* could identify every article I have read in the past six months and how I (and many others) surfed from one type of article to another. Through experiments on its website, the Associated Press can identify what kinds of headlines attract more readers and how readers link from one subject to another.

In 1998 David Hart published a new book, *Forged Consensus,* about the development of technology policy in midcentury. Hart can potentially pay online book retailers for the names, addresses, and e-mail addresses of everyone in the Eighth District who has bought his book online. (It would be a very small list.) Through several online bookstores, Hart can also conceivably purchase information about everyone in the Eighth District who has bought "environmental" books over the past six months. The Belmont book buyers might be a perfect audience to hear about Hart's concerns over the incinerator.

After identifying likely voters and acquiring their e-mail addresses, candidate Hart can build a sense of community among the e-mail users by asking them to become involved in campaign events close to their homes. People like to be asked for favors from politicians if they have an issue or personal background in common. There is an old adage in campaigning: "It is better to receive than to give." A candidate who asks for someone's help in a campaign has most likely received a vote, too, because the person who gives time to a campaign has invested in that candidate's victory. In campaigns, small commitments of time or money are exceptionally valuable, and carefully constructed e-mail lists can help someone like David Hart identify whom to ask for help.

Recruiting Campaign Resources

As we have seen, virtually all U.S. Senate candidates with websites in 2000 used the web to solicit funds and recruit volunteers. Campaign contributors know no boundaries, and the web makes identifying potential issue-specific donors fairly easy. Again, with a web search engine, one could perform a free targeted search of all websites mentioning various words. For Hart, we might search for "'Incinerator' AND 'Environment' AND 'Against.'" When I ran that search in July 1998, I found 203 separate websites mentioning those three words in combination. They were all potential Hart allies. Since 1998, of course, the number of websites has mushroomed. The identical search for "'Incinerator' AND 'Environment' AND 'Against'" conducted in July 2001 yielded 26,400 websites mentioning those three words in combination.

For a simple fundraising gambit, David Hart can send a mass mailing to every David Hart in the phone book nationwide. Using Switchboard.com in July 1998, I found more than sixteen hundred David Harts, with addresses and phone numbers, in less than twenty seconds—and for free.

The search engine 411.com quickly identified 659 separate e-mail accounts registered to David Hart worldwide, and we could do a targeted e-mail to that list in less than twenty minutes. There are thirty-seven David Harts in Massachusetts alone, many who would be thrilled to send $20 to their namesake for Congress.

It takes far less than a $20 contribution to catch a voter in the web. Once someone contributes any small amount, say $5, that person makes a psychological commitment to seeing the candidate win. In most campaigns, $5 matters little, and a solid House campaign would cost David Hart more than $500,000. The importance of the small campaign contributions is in mobilizing voters and securing their psychological investment in the outcome.

Where do the web viewers come from who might make small contributions? They are not likely to stumble across the site, and web pollution is becoming more and more severe. Rather, David Hart has to send highly selective potential voters links to his website, using the identifying techniques discussed in the foregoing account. The more exclusive and "by invitation only" the site appears to be, the more likely web-weary voters are to tune in to it.

Communicating within the Campaign

David Hart's campaign is ahead of its time: in addition to a state-of-the-art narrowcasting website, he maintains a separate website for his own campaign volunteers and coordinators. This site may prove critical in coordinating events across the district and in quickly sharing strategic information.

For campaign workers on the bottom rung, working for a candidate can be a solitary and alienating enterprise. Volunteers go door to door answering scattered questions from voters, though these volunteers may never have met the candidate and often use obsolete campaign materials. With a campaign intranet, the huge gulf between door-knocking volunteers and the candidate can be bridged. Volunteers can be included in discussions and can share observations up the hierarchy much more quickly than in past campaigns.

That is David Hart's plan. His web intranet (password protected and with increased security the closer one gets to strategic documents) is updated daily with information about his campaign. Campaign schedules are modified almost hourly, so his staff can see when he will arrive at schools, picnics, and the like. From his volunteers, he tracks the placement of signs in neighborhoods and quickly thanks volunteers for every door knock and campaign rally. It is not so much that David Hart forges a consensus within his campaign early and then sticks with it. Rather, he continually updates his strategy and personnel to gauge the consensus in his campaign and to keep spirits high. By 2004 congressional campaigns will deploy volunteers into the field for the usual door knocking, but those volunteers will hold Palm Pilots or other small data organizers that will be linked to the Internet, showing maps for walking and texts for talking.

David Hart did not run for Congress in 1998 and probably never will. Still, his could have been a model campaign. Some campaigns, notably Tom Campbell's race for the U.S. House in California and Jessie Ventura's gubernatorial run in Minnesota, have used the web's full potential. The web itself is always changing, and its "full potential" will grow with each election cycle.

We owe Elaine Kamarck a debt for detailing the beginning of the political web, noting not only the percentage of campaigns using the web but, more important, how the web was used in 1998 and 2000. The electronic brochure is the dominant image in her 1998 benchmark, but we have seen rapid innovations since then. Many of those innovations are detailed at PoliticsOnline.com or recorded in the Library of Congress–sponsored campaign archive at Alexa.com.

Although the web is unlikely to change the way members of Congress deliberate, it is already changing the ways they run for office. By 2008 the web will be ubiquitous in congressional campaigns as candidates follow the lead of retail marketers in identifying specific voters, narrowing their messages, and communicating within their campaign organizations. Today a typical campaign's organization chart includes a campaign manager, a treasurer, a press manager, and a volunteer coordinator. Tomorrow a new position will be listed among the campaign's leaders: web coordinator. The web will be that central to tomorrow's campaign, and we will come to think of the computer—with it's dynamic links to data and voters—as the new "political machine."

Notes

1. Kathy Goldschmidt, "E-mail Overload in Congress: Managing a Communications Crisis," Congressional Management Foundation, Alexandria, Virginia, April 2001.

2. Sonia Tita Puopolo, "Senate Campaign Web Sites in the 2000 Elections," Harvard University, April 2001.

3. John W. Kingdon, *Candidates for Office: Beliefs and Strategies* (Random House, 1968).

4. Elaine Ciulla Kamarck, "Campaigning on the Internet in the Elections of 1998," in Elaine Ciulla Kamarck and Joseph S. Nye Jr., eds., *Democracy.com? Governance in a Networked World* (Hollis, N.H.: Hollis Publishing, 1999).

5. Steven M. Schneider, "Congressional Candidate Web Sites in Campaign 2000," Annenberg Public Policy Center, January 2000.

6. Doug Bailey, interview with the author, Cambridge, Massachusetts, April 19, 2001.

8

JANE E. FOUNTAIN

Toward a Theory of Federal Bureaucracy for the Twenty-First Century

THE INTERNET PROMISES vast changes in American government that range from Internet voting to interactive online services for the public to virtual diplomacy. As a vehicle for disjunctive change in communication, coordination, and control, the Internet and related information technologies make possible new and exciting developments in operations, regulation, and enforcement. In spite of its revolutionary power, the potential benefits of the Internet, and its potential perils, will be strongly influenced by the current organizations and institutions of government, for it is within the constraints posed by these structural arrangements that government actors make decisions and information networks that connect to form the World Wide Web are designed, developed, and used.[1]

One of the most intriguing and important questions for scholars and practitioners concerns the structural transformation currently taking place within and across government agencies, the part of government political scientists refer to as the bureaucracy. The intrigue stems from the potential for developing new organizational arrangements that will use the information-processing potential of the Internet and related information technologies. The importance for government arises because such a fundamental change in the structure of bureaucracy bears on central concepts of governance such as accountability, task specialization, and jurisdiction.

Some theorists and futurists have suggested replacements for bureaucracy, including networks, markets, and even self-organizing systems. Approximately a decade ago, as the Internet began to be widely used, others suggested that the nation-state itself would be replaced by a variety of subnational, supranational, and transnational forms of governance. For the foreseeable future, at least the next twenty-five years, it is unlikely that bureaucracy will be superceded by other forms of organization. Moreover, evidence is accumulating that the nation-state not only retains its importance but has taken on new roles as globalization continues. If a new dominant form is emerging to replace bureaucracy, it is not evident just what it is.

Looking back in time, it is useful to place bureaucracy and the modern American state in historical context. The modern American state is a child of the industrial revolution. As the political scientist Stephen Skowronek has observed, the American bureaucratic state was built from a nation of parties and courts. It was born during the final decades of the nineteenth century and the first two decades of the twentieth century. Although the term *bureaucracy* has come to connote much that is inefficient and ineffective about government, it is important to remember that bureaucracy replaced patronage appointments with a professional civil service and, through a protracted series of political negotiations, substituted merit for political loyalty as the key measure of fitness for employment in the professional public service.[2]

There is little theory and no coherent research program within the discipline of political science that seeks to account for the potential or likely effects of major changes in information processing on the bureaucracy. This silence is curious given that during the past two decades, in popular writing and in political practice, many actors have been engaged in "breaking down," "abolishing," and "bashing" bureaucracy. Indeed, the stillness of political scientists on this matter has contributed to a verbal sleight of hand. Rather than use the term *bureaucracy* in its accurate meaning, political and media actors have shifted its definition to mean an organizational form productive of a set of inferior, outmoded processes and outputs. It is not even clear whether one should speak in terms of a postbureaucratic government or of an evolutionary adaptation, or modernization, of bureaucracy.

Political science requires a theory of bureaucracy that accounts for far-reaching, fundamental advances in information processing and a sustained, coherent research program to develop such a theoretical perspective. This chapter outlines the elements of such a research program. It is difficult to argue against the importance and centrality of the bureaucratic form throughout twentieth-century American government. The structure and its constituent processes are largely responsible for the production of binding collective decisions and coordination of policy implementation. If changes in information technology have serious implications for bureaucracy, then theorists must account for such a modification in underlying assumptions regarding information processing.

A useful starting point for a theory of information-based bureaucracy is provided within current bureaucratic and organizational theory. At minimum, an adequate theory must offer guidance to structure systematic research efforts. It should direct the attention of theorists to aspects of the terrain that are important. For the moment, I put aside the requirement for predictive power. Let us first decide on the variables of importance. Adequate theory also guides development of new policy tools, including organizational and program design, to foster improvements in government performance, accountability, and responsiveness.

It is impossible to sensibly discuss how information technology affects the bureaucratic paradigm without returning to the roots of that paradigm, the Weberian bureaucracy. This approach, although less exciting than intellectual excursions into cyberspace and sweeping speculation on the society of the future, provides an important starting point for the development of theory.

Modern Officialdom: Fundamental Properties of Weberian Bureaucracy

Although Max Weber describes bureaucracy as an ideal type, he argues several times in his voluminous output that bureaucracy is the only form of organization able to cope with the complexity of modern enterprise.[3] His delineation of the chief elements of bureaucracy has been central to conceptual understanding of the form and the role of the bureaucrat. The extended quotation that follows, delineating the "characteristics of modern bureaucracy," establishes the definition of bureaucracy used in this analysis.

Modern officialdom functions in the following manner:

I. There is the principle of official *jurisdictional areas*, which are generally ordered by rules, that is, by laws or administrative regulations. This means:

(1) The regular activities required for the purposes of the bureaucratically governed structure are assigned as official duties.

(2) The authority to give the commands required for the discharge of these duties is distributed in a stable way and is strictly delimited by rules. . . .

(3) . . . Only persons who qualify under general rules are employed.

In the sphere of the state these three elements constitute a bureaucratic *agency*, in the sphere of the private economy they constitute a bureaucratic *enterprise*. Bureaucracy, thus understood, is fully developed in political . . . communities only in the modern state, and in the private economy only in the most advanced institutions of capitalism. . . .

II. The principles of *office hierarchy* and of channels of appeal [or "levels of graded authority" in a different translation][4] . . . stipulate a clearly established system of super- and subordination in which there is a supervision of the lower offices by the higher ones. . . .

III. The management of the modern office is based upon written documents (the "files"), which are preserved in their original or draft form, and upon a staff of subaltern officials and scribes of all sorts. The body of officials working in an agency along with the respective apparatus of material implements and the files, make up a *bureau*. . . .

IV. Office management, at least all specialized office management—and such management is distinctly modern—usually presupposes thorough training in a field of specialization. . . .

V. When the office is fully developed, official activity demands the *full working capacity* of the official. . . . Formerly the normal state of affairs was the reverse: Official business was discharged as a secondary activity.

VI. The management of the office follows *general rules*, which are more or less stable, more or less exhaustive, and which can be learned. Knowledge of these rules represents a special technical expertise which the officials possess. It involves jurisprudence, administrative or business management.

The reduction of modern office management to rules is deeply embedded in its very nature.[5]

Jurisdiction

Weber offers, in the first characteristic of bureaucracy, the kernels from which theorists have developed the powerful concepts of division of labor,

functional differentiation, and clear jurisdictional boundaries. One of the
chief effects of advances in information technology on bureaucratic organization has been the ability to structure information using information
systems rather than through strict delineation of role and organizational
subunit. Professional and operational roles will continue, but they have
become broader and more fluid. Recent major revisions to the descriptions
and classification system of civil service positions provide evidence for the
current restructuring of roles within the federal bureaucracy. Similarly,
jurisdictional boundaries have changed character. Although they have not
disappeared, boundaries have become more permeable.[6]

Hierarchy

Weber's second characteristic, hierarchy, forms the essence of bureaucracy
for many theorists. Herbert Simon, a key figure in both bureaucratic theory and automated information processing, traces the dominance of hierarchy through a variety of natural as well as social systems.[7] Simon argues
that hierarchy represents a structural form that encompasses and enables
the decomposability of complex problems. The ability to factor complex
problems and then to assign the results to specialists is the chief reason that
complex organization—bureaucracy—supercedes other forms of organization. Simon offers as evidence of the superiority of complex organization
not only greater efficiency of output but also the exceptional robustness of
decomposable systems able to withstand and recover from interruptions
and disruptions from a variety of sources.

Information technology, primarily in the form of shared databases and
electronic communications, has promoted greater use of cross-functional
groups and teams at both the operational and professional levels. The predominance of these problem-solving groups diminishes the centrality of
hierarchy. The ability to place information and computing power at the
operational levels of a hierarchy while making results rapidly transparent at
upper levels underlies current capacity to devolve decisionmaking to operational personnel. Thus, "empowerment," often viewed from the perspective of human relations, may be understood as a structural (and cultural)
artifact of technological advancement.

Theorists as early as the 1950s predicted the demise of middle management as a direct result of mainframe computer use in complex organizations.[8] Their forecast was based on the clear obsolescence of middle

management tasks in light of office automation. That their prediction took more than thirty years to come to fruition merely illuminates the difficulty of making deep structural modifications in complex organizations. The lag between technological and social change often is substantial. But a high proportion of positions lost through the downsizing of federal employees at the outset of the National Performance Review, the major government reform initiative undertaken by the Clinton administration, consisted of middle management.

In spite of some "flattening" and loosening of command and control systems, hierarchy remains central to most complex organizations. The important question for students of bureaucracy concerns the optimal, or appropriate, types of hierarchy in information-based organizations. Reductions in levels within the chain of command in several bureaucracies signal the natural experiment currently under way. The rapid rise of scholarly interest in network forms, both within organizations and among them, has obscured the fact that networks continue to rest largely on a hierarchical base. Changes in hierarchy and its function in the bureaucracy have implications for the structure and practice of authority as well as for other properties, practices, and politics that flow from command and control systems of decisionmaking.

The "Files" and the Staff

The third chief characteristic according to Weber, the "files," constitutes an equally important departure from the idiosyncratic, personalized office. As bureaucracy became central to the modern state, for example, tax collectors could no longer individually define their operational methods. Written rules and the evolution of standard procedures, stored in the files, formed the basis for the rationalization of the state and the economy.

Digital files structured as shared databases place data and information throughout bureaucracy rather than in the hands of actors assigned specific functions and at specific levels. A notable result has been the detachment of information from individuals holding a particular role. This fundamental structural shift has important implications for the meaning of the statement "information is power." Much has been written concerning the assumed democratization expected to occur as a result of information sharing and transparency.

Bureaucratic Neutrality

Weber also articulates the role of the bureaucrat as neutral with respect to organizational direction, impersonal with respect to application of law and administrative regulations, and expert in the conduct of a particular, clearly defined office. Although several theorists have discounted the notion of bureaucratic neutrality,[9] the concept remains normatively powerful and a key feature of civil service professionalism. The chief contemporary changes in the bureaucrat's role have derived from the increasingly cross-functional and enlarged character of many positions in organizations in which project teams form and disband according to agency requirements.

General Rules

Finally, Weber outlines the rationalization of bureaus and offices increasingly ordered by rules and procedures. Weber's then radical perspective captures the transition from patriarchal, patrimonial, intensely political, and personal systems of organization to the rational, impersonal, efficient, rule-based bureaucracy currently under siege. Information-based organization is equally, if not more strongly, rule based and more highly rationalized. However, rules embedded within information systems become less visible and seemingly less constraining to bureaucratic discretion. Embedded rules will increasingly replace overt supervisory control. Indeed, in many cases, so-called empowerment represents little more than a shift from overt to covert control through embedded rule systems and peer groups.[10]

Bureaucratic Transformation: Three Levels of Analysis

Theory must be sensitive to levels of analysis. Three levels are important for this analysis. Weberian properties focus implicitly on the bureaucratic structure as a whole, thereby missing intraorganizational (individual, group, subunit) and interorganizational phenomena. I flag some of the key implications of information processing advancement for the federal bureaucracy at each level. The main point is to extend the focus of Weberian analysis to capture effects that range from those operating primarily at the level of the individual to those that transcend the boundaries of the bureaucracy.

At the intraorganizational level, effects on individuals, groups, and sub-units are found. I note substantial change in the design of work, an area addressed partially through process redesign efforts initiated as part of the Clinton administration's National Performance Review and continuing in the Bush administration. Knowledge workers and knowledge work have replaced simple, repetitive clerical tasks required in paper-based bureaucracy. Caseworkers, whose desktop computing capacity provides access to several databases and powerful analytic tools, perform work previously disaggregated into several positions. In some cases, automated tools allow relatively unsophisticated employees to make sophisticated evaluations. Task integration owing to information technology has resulted in a collapse in the number of job categories and simplification of the position classification system in the federal bureaucracy.

The information revolution carries with it a host of human resource implications, such as the appropriate design of careers, reward systems, and performance measures in the bureaucracy. As command and control decision systems have modernized, a stream of secondary effects requires systematic attention. These include modifications to supervisory roles, transformation of hierarchical relations, and, at a deep cultural level, modernization of the nature of authority structures and systems.

At the organizational level, major advances in information technologies have led to several structural changes. The dominance of the manager, a direct outgrowth of bureaucratic development, formed a dominant focus of scholarly attention after World War II.[11] Technology has substituted machines for labor, leading to a sharp decrease in traditional middle-management positions. An equally important, though less well recognized, effect lies in the enormous number of new positions required to develop, maintain, and service the information-based organization and the information society. Growth of information technology–related positions is predicted to vastly outstrip labor market supply during the next decade.[12] Scholarly attention during that time may usefully be directed toward the growing dominance and influence of systems analysts within information-based bureaucracy.

Information technology diminishes, and in some cases eliminates, time and distance barriers, leading to the proliferation of work groups whose members are geographically distributed, to new agency arrangements, and to new types of government services. One of the most important developments has been the growth of cross-functional arrangements. These arrangements exist both in human form, as cross-functional teams, and in automated form, as process redesign—the consolidation and streamlining of tasks previously accomplished sequentially. In many cases, "business" units (responsible for particular products or services) have been created in place of functional units.

Finally, interorganizational-level change has been catalyzed as the external boundaries of agencies and other organizations have become more permeable. Agencies have increased partnerships with other agencies, with private and nonprofit entities, and with customers to gain efficiencies through improved problem solving and more effective design of production and operations. Although this phenomenon is best known through the efficiencies gained from contracting for business services, a comparable level of partnership activity characterizes many government activities.[13] Through the use of electronic data interchange, agencies have overcome the costs of coordination to gain its efficiencies: reduced paperwork, increased speed and accuracy of transactions, improved control of inventories and suppliers, strengthened channel control, improved relationships with customers, resource and risk sharing, and integration and synergy without ownership.[14]

This inquiry thus far has classified some of the chief properties of information technologies that either presently affect or are likely to affect the bureaucracy. It has also outlined some of the chief modifications to bureaucracy in terms comparable to those used by Weber. I have done this because theory development requires more precise language than is typically found in discussions of technology and government. The invention of new terms provides excitement but obscures theory.

Implications of Technology for Capacity and Control

One more lens is required through which to view the implications of the information revolution on the bureaucracy. Although bureaucratic theorists think in terms of structure and process, typical discourse in public administration and management uses a closely related but different terminology. It focuses on the activities of the bureaucracy and their achievement through agency capacity and control. Weber's concepts represent antecedents of capacity and control. Theoretical development, therefore, invites examination of technological change in light of these properties of the administrative state.

The National Performance Review was criticized roundly by public administration scholars. This criticism reflects the lack of theory adequate to guide analysis of technological change and bureaucratic behavior. Misled by rhetoric touting empowerment, critics ignored fundamental technological change and its implications.

For example, as part of an extended critical essay on the National Performance Review, Gerald Garvey asked,

> How do you retain control when you eliminate bureaucracy, *whose essence is control achieved through the codification of knowledge, the inculcation of habits, and the structuring of hierarchical authority?* The answer may be you do not retain control. Or, if the existing system of controls is too deeply entrenched, you just talk about eliminating bureaucracy—citing anecdotal instead of systemic evidences of radical change—instead of really doing it.

This critique follows from well-known principles of public administration. Administrative behavior must satisfy the dual requirements of capacity and control. Capacity indicates the ability of an administrative unit to achieve its objectives efficiently. Control refers to accountability owing to "higher authority, most particularly to elected representatives in the legislative branch."[15]

Democratic accountability, at least since the Progressive Era, has relied upon hierarchical control, control by superiors of subordinates along a chain of command that stretches from the apex of the organization, the politically appointed agency head, and beyond to the members of Congress down to operational-level employees. The reform effort that began with the National Performance Review, according to Garvey and most critics, "involves the substitution of bottom-up control, that is, control of officials in their day-to-day work by those officials' 'customers,' the citizens whom they serve."[16]

The scientific managers of the early and middle twentieth century developed governmental structures according to the scientific method of Frederick Taylor and the normative explanations of bureaucratic behavior developed by Max Weber.[17] The bureaucratic structure of modern organizations in the private and public sectors is a lineal descendent of Taylorism. It solved the problem of how to achieve capacity in complex problem solving requiring coordination of a large number of subtasks and functions while retaining control over a disparate enterprise.

Political scientists typically explain the rise of the modern administrative state as a response to industrialization during the industrial revolution in the United States.[18] However, organizational forms developed by state and industry also were rendered possible by the technological achievements that underlay the industrial revolution. The steam engine, the telegraph, the telephone, and early adding machines all made possible bureaucracy, as well as the interorganizational forms underlying business and government, by allowing the development of vertical integration and spatially dispersed headquarters and field organizations. Technological developments did not determine these forms in an inevitable fashion, but they made them possible and, in some cases, were completely logical developments.

Information technology differs from other technologies in its capacity as a general-purpose manipulator of symbols used in all types of work. It resembles the steam engine, in the generality and breadth of its applications, and is having effects on a scale similar to that of the steam engine during the industrial revolution. Information technology is different from other types of technology because it affects production of goods and services (or capacity) as well as coordination and control.[19]

One indicator of the tremendous applications of and demand for information technology is cost. The cost of information processing has decreased enormously during the past twenty years and is projected to continue to drop dramatically. As the economics of information technology continue to drive down its costs, its effects should continue to proliferate throughout government. Current estimates show cost-performance ratios to be declining at a rate of 20 to 30 percent a year.[20]

I have already briefly noted the lag between advances in information technology and bureaucracy. In spite of stunning examples of innovation in the federal government as well as in other sectors, empirical studies find few examples of fundamental organizational change to date either in the private or public sectors. I have argued in previous research that institutionalized norms and values, bureaucratic politics, and tightly coupled routines are highly resistant to change. Indeed, organizations often appear to change technology, rather than their own practices, by using or enacting technology in suboptimal ways that allow the status quo to continue.[21] It is easy to discount the deep political and social adjustments that have to occur for organizations to leverage the potential afforded by information technologies.

Five processes underpin and influence organizational capacity and control: production, coordination, control, direction, and integration. Information technologies affect and potentially reshape each process and, in doing so, have the ability to restructure capacity and control in government organizations.

Production

A key aspect of production, or capacity, in government affected by information technology is intellectual production or knowledge work. "The degree to which a person can be affected by [changes in information technology depends upon] how much of the work is based on information—that is, information on what product to make or what service to deliver and how to do it (the production task), as well as when to do it and in conjunction with whom (the coordination task)."[22] Government officials who develop loans and other financial instruments, provide counseling, write contracts, regulations, and legislation are involved in intellectual production. Other knowledge workers in the federal government include engineers, designers, budget analysts, and lawyers. The knowledge worker adds value to information.

Clerical tasks, of which there are an enormous number in government, are affected by information technology. These tasks, often classified as "information work," include accounts receivable, billing, and accounts payable. Thus social security administration, tax administration, welfare disbursements, student loan programs, and a large number of other programs have been transformed by information technology—or have that potential easily at hand.

A major potential advance for government concerns the application of information technology to knowledge production in the form of workstations for those who assemble qualitative products, such as loans, letters of credit, and contracts, and for those who design "soft" products, including legislation or new software. The application of information technology to knowledge work has been much slower than its application to physical production. Production processes involved in knowledge work—for example, professional expertise, research, creativity, and judgment—are less well understood and far less easily routinized. Experience with knowledge-based programs or expert systems demonstrates that rule-based systems work well as aids to clearly defined problems but tend to produce poor results outside well-bounded domains. Organizations, particularly in government, have been slower to exploit information technology in the area for this reason.

Coordination

Much of what federal agencies do falls under the category of coordination. Communication networks enabled by information technology are being built within subunits and agencies as well as among agencies and countries and constitute essential elements of much-needed information infrastructure. The National Performance Review itself was sustained and disseminated in part through a telecommunications network linking federal employees. The Internet and its predecessor, ARPANET, developed by the Advanced Research Projects Agency (ARPA) of the U.S. Department of Defense, are among the largest networks connecting government employees and millions of other users. As an outcome of Information Technology Initiative 6 of the National Performance Review, the prototype of an integrated trade data system was negotiated and developed. The system was an effort to standardize and link trade-related data among more than sixty federal agencies and bureaus with responsibilities for trade policy and administration. Lack of consistent standards continues to inhibit the proliferation of communication networks both within and outside government. As standards are negotiated, the growth of electronic networks should increase dramatically.

Information technologies potentially alter coordination through their effects on the relations among information, distance, time, and memory. First, distance becomes far less relevant with regard to information flow. This has implications for partnerships and the location of work. Second, time becomes more fluid as federal organizations and their partners in different time zones shift work to gain efficiencies. Store-and-forward systems and common databases make time far less relevant. For example, the Social Security Administration shifts telephone calls dialed into its teleservice centers from one time zone to another in order to expand its service to the public beyond the typical federal workday.

Third, organizational memory, in the form of shared databases, collects data from and provides it to all authorized points in agencies as well as maintains information in easily retrievable and malleable form over time. Organizational memory is an important aspect of coordination. Agency and interagency databases constitute a "memory" that can be accessed systematically and analyzed to benefit administration and future decision-making. For example, personnel databases may be used to identify skill mixes, possible succession plans, and candidates for positions. Shared databases containing retrievable, manageable information affect coordination through their potential to allow decisionmakers to better detect patterns.

These three aspects of coordination—time, distance, and memory—make it possible for agencies to establish and use teams whose members work in disparate locations, whose work is conducted without face-to-face meetings, and whose production is shared throughout the team's existence. Telecommunications networks allow decisionmakers within the administrative apparatus to locate nearly any information, any time, anywhere, and in nearly any format. This coordination capacity depends upon an infrastructure that is being put into place at different rates in different agencies. With this telecommunications infrastructure comes the ability to virtually link employees and work both within agencies and, increasingly, across agencies and entities.

Control

Two aspects of control are important to consider in relation to public management. First, measurement of agency or program performance against a set of criteria is critical to control, although sometimes devilishly difficult to implement in government. The second aspect of measurement involves timely, clear, and accurate feedback of measured results to decisionmakers, interpretation of those results, and subsequent decisions based on interpreted feedback.

Information technology cannot determine the appropriate performance measures for agencies, but it embeds routines in programs and procedures that make data collection easier, data collation automatic, and report generation in a variety of forms simple. Information technologies rationalize elements of tasks more powerfully than standard-operating-procedures manuals and first-line supervisors are capable of doing. Software applications make clear to federal employees those aspects of their tasks that are discretionary; and databases collect information so that control is far greater than is possible in a traditional bureaucracy because the actions of most employees are captured electronically and easily stored and analyzed in terms of quantity and some qualities of output. So information-based organizations codify knowledge and inculcate habits in a somewhat different, but much more powerful, fashion than is possible in traditional bureaucracy. The control problem in government has never been easier to manage.

The marginal discretion granted to employees is meant in part to enhance "customer service" or empowerment or some other human relations objective. But greater discretion also is critical to prevent technologically constrained jobs from becoming completely uninteresting to employees. Given the capability to control employee behavior and outputs to such a great extent, added discretion at the margins achieves benefits without loss of discipline.

It is certain that a solid core of hierarchy and functional specialization will remain in information-based organizations. The control apparatus that required multiple layers in the chain of command has been greatly simplified, however, with gains in accountability, through information technology. With information systems that render employee behavior largely transparent, hierarchical authority is relieved of the task of physically observing employees. Shirking is obvious, as is greater output, in a transparent system. Hierarchical authority takes on the more important task of setting the direction in turbulent environments, keeping officials current with environmental changes, and ensuring the alignment of task, technology, human resources, and goals.

Control systems traditionally serve three functions. First, they help decisionmakers use resources more effectively by providing feedback, thereby making the production process more "visible." Second, they serve to put disparate units and divisions of the agency in line with agency goals. Finally, they provide data for decisionmaking at the strategic and operational levels.[23] Information technology has provided the potential for more than efficiency gains in existing processes and systems. It has created a set of new tools for collecting, managing, and using information. One of the challenges for gaining these new capacities lies in linking program managers, control staff, and information resource managers in agencies in order to put information into the most valuable locations.

Data storage is relatively inexpensive. To sustain innovation, the federal government should "reinvent" all information systems that stymie the efforts of users to manage information and that make information retrieval slow and complex. Those frictions are outmoded. Information-based control systems should be able to respond to changes in external conditions. Decisionmakers can use information-based control systems to decide where information should appear and in what form. For example, data collected at remote field locations is as easily available at headquarters as it is in those field locations and may be transferred without having to travel through several hierarchical layers. In other cases, the value of information generated at headquarters might be enhanced by making it available to operating managers in field locations. One of the important benefits of automated battlefield management systems for the U.S. Army, to note one example, is the ability to provide the same data to each battalion or brigade commander in a division nearly simultaneously, thereby providing a consistent view of the battlefield to each decisionmaker.

Information technology renders the tension between centralization and decentralization obsolete. Data can be placed at either or both headquarters and field locations in forms useful to decisionmakers at several levels. So a critical management task becomes deciding which data are needed at various organizational locations, how timely those data should be, and in what forms they would be most useful to the decisionmakers who will use them.

In some cases, centralization of data collected from branch offices may be useful. Data that have been filtered through several hierarchical layers are less useful because "bad news" is routinely filtered out of aggregate numbers and because the data are often outdated by the time reports reach headquarters staff. Information systems allow for objective data reduction and near-real-time transmission. Alternatively, if field personnel lack the information to make effective operational decisions, then agencies may benefit from decentralization of some data. When performance incentives are linked to control systems through shared information, the effect on performance is powerful and meaningful. Many managers perform suboptimally because they either are not fully aware of agency goals, lack the informational resources to make intelligent decisions, or lack motivation because their incentives fail to match their externally supplied objectives.[24]

Integration

Reengineering, a process redesign method widely attempted in the federal government, captures some of the coordination and integration capacities of information technology. It is limited, however, by several constraints. First, integration of production processes depends largely on the telecommunications infrastructure available to make integration feasible. Second, some skill in work design, management of change, and leadership is necessary both to design the integration and, more important, to implement it.

Integration is actually a broader, more powerful concept than business process redesign, or reengineering. It can be classified into four levels. First, integration can occur within the operational processes of an agency. This is the typical application of reengineering in which teams are formed around one process linked by a local area network. Agencies have improved capacity greatly by breaking down barriers between functional areas and, more modestly, by reducing barriers between employee classifications. The increased ability to coordinate provided by information technologies makes the traditional need for narrow task specialization far less important.

Second, agencies have a growing ability to electronically integrate production that lies across organizational boundaries. This capacity greatly speeds the flow of information and services across organizations. The ability to integrate processes in this way relies on electronic data interchange. Organizational boundaries in information-based organizations are highly permeable with respect to these interorganizational arrangements. Third, agencies can subcontract and outsource larger pieces of production processes to other state and local governments, private firms, and non-profit organizations. Information technology enables these arrangements by greatly reducing coordination costs, by standardizing data elements across sites, and by making communication easier across organizational boundaries. Finally, information technology has made electronic markets possible.

Each of the levels of integration reduces coordination costs and increases the effectiveness of coordination by eliminating the need for buffers—"inventories" of supplies, information, and expertise—and by pooling expertise.[25] The capacity to provide resources where they are needed when they are needed removes time lags (or wait times) and further reduces the need for buffers.

These four types of integration require a threshold level of information technology infrastructure in communications capacity, data standardization, applications software, and human expertise.[26] Major increases in capacity, coordination, and control as a result of integration still reside largely in the future and await sufficient infrastructure.[27]

The ability to integrate in various ways is changing and will continue to change the contours of government, the relation between competition and collaboration among actors, and government-business relations. To cite one example, the Internal Revenue Service has created the capacity to receive electronic filing of individual income tax returns prepared by tax preparation firms. The shift to electronic processing creates enormous efficiency gains within the IRS. Moreover, this integration creates opportunities for lending or borrowing approximately $70 billion, thereby driving a set of new opportunities among several actors in the financial services business. This example also highlights the importance of the federal government's role with regard to setting standards because of the potential impact of federal decisions on the competitive structure of most industries.

Direction and Transformation

To understand the effect of information technology on capacity and control, the executive functions of direction and transformation must be considered. Direction involves sensing environmental occurrences, including changes that may affect a policy or program and public response to governmental action. It also involves interpretation of these data and decisionmaking designed to respond to feedback from the environment. The information technology systems involve strategic planning systems as well as systems to capture customer feedback.

The enormous potential of information technologies to both quantitatively and, more important, qualitatively improve and enlarge capacity should prompt agencies to rethink their missions. Many operational decisions are based on existing capacity. New capacities should prompt rethinking. Without direct competitive pressure, the federal government has an opportunity, but relatively little pressure some would say, to rethink its operations. However, I have argued elsewhere that citizens expect transactions with their government to be roughly as efficient as those with private sector organizations.[28]

Developments within information technology have spawned a progression in some organizations from automation to information to transformation. Automation has occurred, and continues to occur, as production costs are reduced by automating work formerly carried out by people. Automation of traditional paper processing is proceeding in the federal government but needs to progress much further. Tracking tools, scanners, and bar codes have greatly improved knowledge of the status of processes and shipments in agencies as disparate as the Immigration and Naturalization Service, which processes applications for residency and citizenship, and the Defense Industrial Supply Center of the Defense Logistics Agency, which processes purchasing requests from the military services. Those workers who are not replaced by technology require new skill sets to work closely with information technologies. Their work has become more abstract, less tactile, more mathematical, less heuristic.

The same technologies that potentially reduce production costs, however, also, in most cases, provide the capacity to capture and systematically organize information as a by-product of the process. Shoshana Zuboff coined the term "informate" to denote this capacity created by information technology and, until recently, largely ignored by automation efforts.[29] Informating processes not only implies capturing and generating useful information but also requires human resources and new internal processes to make use of this new information. Both operating-level personnel and managers must modify their skill sets to recognize useful patterns, exceptions to patterns, and information that may be usefully transmitted to others.

Indeed, information generated by technologies used in government has spawned entire businesses. The Defense Department sells maps and other information collected by sensors, satellites, and related technologies. In other cases, information collected by the government, and paid for by taxpayers, is packaged and marketed by private firms. The amount of valuable information generated by the government will increase dramatically as information technologies are more fully exploited. The use of that information prompts a set of policy, procedural, and economic questions regarding markets for information.

The third and most ambitious step, transformation, refers to organizations' use of information technologies to build internal and external infrastructures for communication, information transfer, and more that have taken advantage of integrative and coordinative capacities provided by those infrastructural elements. In many cases, new services have been developed, the boundaries of the organization have effectively changed, and work has been substantially redesigned. This level and degree of change, however, has so far been relatively rare in the private as well as public sectors. Technology is a necessary but far from sufficient condition for substantial structural change and redirection. Transformation occurs as a result of several years of knowledgeable, effective executive leadership and investments in technology and human resources.

The potential effects of information technology on capacity, coordination, control, direction, and transformation hint at the potential of information technology to substantially redistribute power, functional responsibilities, and control within and across federal agencies and between the public and private sectors. As coordination costs continue to decline dramatically and economics of scale change through technology, the effects on institutional design will be felt. The "metabolic rate" of administration is increasing in rapidity and quality.[30] Both greater rapidity in information processing and greater interdependence require new administrative systems to measure, reward, and motivate desired behaviors and new skills for operational employees, public managers, and appointed and elected officials.

There appear to be two chief requirements for using information technology to increase capacity, coordination, and control in public administration. The first is difficult: Implementation and use of systems must be optimized to support a set of goals. Agencies often must espouse vague, conflicting goals for political survival. No amount of rationalization, either through performance measures or new technologies, has altered this fundamental political reality. Increased rationalization of information technology is at odds with this political fact. Second, a threshold is crossed when information infrastructure is put into place, allowing for integration in data collection, management, communication, and retrieval. Both a technical infrastructure and a set of standards are required for a high level of coordination to be possible. The sheer scale of many federal operations, in addition to the balkanized culture that characterizes many agencies, creates considerable drag on infrastructure construction and interoperability.

Most agencies have constructed a rag-tag assortment of incompatible systems. Capital investments have been made, but to suboptimal effect. Information resource managers traditionally have held operational, rather than strategic, roles. It is in the domain of information resources management, particularly strategic management of technology, that public managers require development.

Conclusions and Broader Implications

I have presented evidence to argue for the development of a theory of information-based bureaucracy. The line of evidence also supports the second argument of this chapter, namely, that a useful starting point for theory already exists in bureaucratic theory. A series of underlying assumptions regarding the character of information processing require fundamental alteration if we are to understand current efforts to modernize bureaucracy.

Predictive theory is not important to develop at this juncture. First, such development would be premature. Second, this discussion has omitted critical intervening variables that strongly mediate any hypothetical direct effects of information technology on elements of bureaucracy. I have analyzed the role and importance of these intervening variables extensively in the technology enactment framework developed in *Building the Virtual*

State.[31] This chapter simplifies causal analysis to identify and focus on key independent variables that have been neglected by students of government. I have shown several of the enabling properties of information technology in relation to bureaucratic structure and practice but have presented a simplified version of technology enactment.

Weberian bureaucracy is the foundation of the modern state. Its chief properties–official jurisdictional areas, hierarchy, management by "files," and generalized rules–are affected in various and complex ways by the information revolution. It is insufficient, in fact it is inaccurate, to claim that bureaucracy is outmoded. Although greatly altered by changing information technology, each element of bureaucracy remains central.

For many students of government, "the bureaucracy" is a phrase synonymous with the civil service. The bureaucrat of the information age will require a vastly different set of skills and expertise. The structure of careers and mobility with the Civil Service has already been altered as a second-order consequence of changes in information technology. Similarly, the incentive structure and behavior of key groups within the bureaucracy— task forces, interagency working groups, committees, and the like—have been irrevocably altered, with implications for policy and politics.

Attention to the interorganizational level of analysis and the implications of technological change illuminates key phenomena. The level of contracting available to agencies is directly related to the technical means available to coordinate across jurisdictions. Recent emphasis on partnership also represents a form of coordination not available without current information technologies in place. The new public management emphasizes the economics of organization but requires additional attention to the economics of information to account for the explosive growth of partnerships and networks.

The perspective on capacity and control presented in this chapter provides a counterargument to critics of recent government reform efforts such as the National Performance Review. Absent an understanding of technological change and its effects on capacity and control, students of bureaucracy can make little sense of either the rhetoric or reality of changes in human relations, such as empowerment, increased employee discretion, and customer service. Rules embedded in hardware and software form a system of control unimaginable in paper-based systems. Discretion in an embedded rule regime is highly constrained.

Information technology affects production, coordination, and control—the nervous system of government. The breadth and importance of these implications have yet to be fully appreciated by researchers or practitioners. Political scientists must develop a political economy of information that accounts for the effects and the enactment of new information and communication technologies.

A theory of information-based bureaucracy should account for stability as well as change in the form of organization that undergirds the modern state. Just as bureaucratic theory, like all theory, accretes through successive refinements, a theory to account for vast changes in the information-processing capacity of the bureaucracy will necessarily evolve during the next several decades. The features of information technology and bureaucracy outlined in this chapter present the basis for a research program to bring bureaucratic theory into the next century.

Notes

1. The argument developed in this chapter is presented in greater detail in Jane E. Fountain, *Building the Virtual State: Information Technology and Institutional Change* (Brookings, 2001).

2. Stephen Skowronek, *Building a New American State: The Expansion of National Administrative Capacities, 1877–1920* (Cambridge University Press, 1982).

3. Max Weber, *Economy and Society,* 2 vols., ed. Guenther Roth and Claus Wittich (University of California Press, 1978).

4. Hans Gerth and C. Wright Mills, eds., *From Max Weber: Essays in Sociology* (Oxford University Press, 1946).

5. Weber, *Economy and Society,* vol. 2., chap. 11, pp. 956–58.

6. This change is addressed later in the chapter.

7. Herbert A. Simon, "The Architecture of Complexity," *Proceedings of the American Philosophical Society,* vol. 106 (December 1962), pp. 467–82.

8. Harold J. Leavitt and Thomas L. Whisler, "Management in the 1980s," *Harvard Business Review* (November–December 1958), pp. 41–48.

9. Among those theorists who at least partially reject the idea of bureaucratic neutrality are Chester Barnard (*The Functions of the Executive* [Harvard University Press, 1948]), James March and Herbert Simon (*Organizations* [John Wiley, 1958]), Anthony Downs (*Inside Bureaucracy* [Boston: Little, Brown, 1967]), and Oliver E. Williamson (*The Economic Institutions of Capitalism* [Free Press, 1985]).

10. See the special issue "Critical Perspectives on Organizational Control," *Administrative Science Quarterly,* vol. 43, no. 2 (1998), especially John M. Jermier, "Introduction: Critical Perspectives on Organizational Control," pp. 235–56, and Graham Sewell, "The Discipline of Teams: The Control of Team-Based Industrial Work through Electronic and Peer Surveillance," pp. 397–428. See also Frederick M. Gordon, "Bureaucracy: Can We Do Better? We Can Do Worse," in Charles Heckscher and Anne Donnellon, eds., *The Post-*

Bureaucratic Organization: New Perspectives on Organizational Change (Thousand Oaks, Calif.: Sage Publications, 1994).

11. See, for example, James Burnham, *The Managerial Revolution* (New York: John Day, 1941); William H. Whyte Jr., *The Organization Man* (Simon and Schuster, 1956).

12. Office of Technology Policy, Technology Administration, *America's New Deficit: The Shortage of Information Technology Workers* (U.S. Department of Commerce, Fall 1997).

13. Jane E. Fountain, "Social Capital: Its Relationship to Innovation in Science and Technology," *Science and Public Policy*, vol. 25, no. 2 (1998), pp. 103-15.

14. See James I. Cash Jr., Robert G. Eccles, Nitin Nohria, and Richard L. Nolan, *Building the Information-Based Organization: Structure, Control, and Information Technologies* (Boston: Irwin, 1994).

15. Gerald Garvey, "False Promises: The NPR in Historical Perspective," in Donald F. Kettl and John J. DiIulio Jr., eds., *Inside the Reinvention Machine: Appraising Governmental Reform* (Brookings, 1995), pp. 91, 87 (emphasis added).

16. Ibid., p. 88. I share concern regarding the customer service metaphor as a tool of government, but my critique differs from that of Garvey; see Jane E. Fountain, "Paradoxes of Public Sector Customer Service," *Governance*, vol. 14, no. 1 (2001), pp. 55-73.

17. Frederick Winslow Taylor, *Principles of Scientific Management* (1911; W. W. Norton, 1967).

18. For an extended analysis, see Skowronek, *Building a New American State*.

19. I am indebted to Joanne Yates, Michael Scott Morton, and other students of information technology and organization at the Massachusetts Institute of Technology for research and analysis, cited in the notes that follow, on the relationship between current information technology and earlier technologies. Michael S. Scott Morton, ed., *The Corporation of the 1990s: Information Technology and Organizational Transformation* (Oxford University Press, 1991).

20. Joanne Yates and Robert I. Benjamin, "The Past and Present as a Window on the Future," in Morton, *The Corporation of the 1990s*.

21. Fountain, *Building the Virtual State*.

22. Yates and Benjamin, "The Past and Present as a Window on the Future."

23. William J. Bruns and F. Warren McFarlan, "Information Technology Puts Power in Control Systems," *Harvard Business Review* (September–October 1987), pp. 89–96.

24. Ibid.

25. Michael Hammer and James Champy, *Reengineering the Corporation* (New York: Harper Business, 1993); Yates and Benjamin, "The Past and Present as a Window on the Future."

26. Regarding the convergence of intelligent transportation and the national information infrastructure, see, for example, Lewis Branscomb and James Keller, eds., *Converging Infrastructures* (MIT Press, 1996).

27. For similar examples at the state level of government, see Jane E. Fountain, with Carlos A. Osorio-Urzua, "Public Sector: First Stage of a Deep Transformation," in Robert Litan and Alice Rivlin, eds., *The Economic Payoff from the Internet Revolution* (Brookings, 2001).

28. Jane E. Fountain, Linda Kaboolian, Steven Kelman, and Jerry Mechling, "Summary, Findings, and Recommendation," in *Customer Service Excellence: Using Information*

Technologies to Improve Service Delivery in Government (Strategic Computing and Telecommunications in the Public Sector Program, John F. Kennedy School of Government, Harvard University, 1993).

29. Shoshana Zuboff, *In the Age of the Smart Machine: The Future of Work and Power* (Basic Books, 1984), p. 10.

30. Yates and Benjamin, "The Past and Present as a Window on the Future," p. 18.

31. Fountain, *Building the Virtual State.*

9

JERRY MECHLING

Information Age Governance: Just the Start of Something Big?

IN THESE FIRST YEARS of the twenty-first century, governments around the world are preparing for e-government. Websites have been created for many government programs, and the push is on for broader and more easily navigated portals. Transactions such as car registration are being offered over the Internet. Politicians and the press are beginning to talk about "digital democracy."

As we pursue the e-government agenda, where do we stand? Have we completed the most important elements, or are we just getting started? Will network technology fundamentally transform government as we have known it or merely lead to modest reforms?

The answer here is that if the e-government agenda were a trip to the moon, we would have just cleared the gantry a few seconds ago. Yes, we have invested some serious money and generated some noise and attention. Yes, we have created movement. But we are still a long way from our final destination. The big opportunities—and the serious threats—still lie ahead. Now is not the time for complacency or for falling asleep at the switch.

The initial progress on e-government has followed a predictable pattern (see figure 9-1). As with most technologies in most settings, the early applications have been decidedly incremental. In essence, the Internet has been used to make services more convenient—available twenty-four hours a day

Figure 9-1. *Trajectory of E-government*

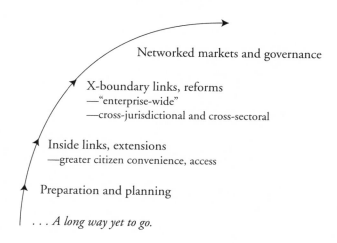

Networked markets and governance

X-boundary links, reforms
—"enterprise-wide"
—cross-jurisdictional and cross-sectoral

Inside links, extensions
—greater citizen convenience, access

Preparation and planning

. . . A long way yet to go.

from home and work and without time-consuming trips to government offices. So far, however, neither the Internet in particular nor computer networking in general has been used much for dramatic improvement in service efficiency, customization, and integration. In addition, we have made scant headway on concerns about the impact of e-government on privacy, security, equity, and the very legitimacy of our institutions of governance. The final success or failure of this trip remains very much yet to be determined.

Shaping and Legitimating Values:
Gently Exploring "Digital Democracy"

Society needs governance to resolve conflicts in a civilized and effective manner. In theory, in a homogeneous society with few interactions, the institutions of governance might require but little power and authority to do their work. However, such a society could hardly be called strong. Economic and military strength depend on a complex division of labor that inevitably produces conflict as well as cooperation. Responding effectively to new threats or opportunities presumes dissatisfaction with the status quo, which in itself also engenders conflict.[1]

The information age is thus creating new challenges for governance by encouraging a more complex division of labor and a flood of new threats and opportunities. In the Confucian sense, these should be "interesting" times. Modern communications are reducing the power of geographic proximity in shaping our sense of community and determining who has the legitimacy needed to govern.[2]

In the longer term, computer-based communications could significantly restructure politics and governance as well as economics. For many people, for example, participation in politics is a secondary concern, at least relative to concerns about self, family, and job. Computer networks, however, are making it more convenient to participate in conversations that were formerly hard to join. This may well lead to new patterns of political communication and participation. More people may find they have the "free time" needed for the conversation of politics. At least conceptually, there may be less reliance on representatives and more on direct decisionmaking by the community.[3] There may also be a need to legitimate communities organized within nongeographic boundaries.[4] For example, the Internet Corporation for Assigned Names and Numbers (ICANN) was formed as a nonprofit corporation whose board represents global stakeholders but not nation-states; though the legitimacy of ICANN's authority has been—and will continue to be—tested, it represents an interesting experiment in governance. The council was designed in the hope that it could respond more quickly (and therefore more effectively) than could a multilateral governmental organization.[5]

Although the visions for digital democracy are often bold, real-world applications have lagged considerably.[6] In some jurisdictions, to be sure, public hearings are taking testimony through videoconferencing, rulemaking bodies are seeking comments over the World Wide Web, and agencies have opened e-mail links to constituents.[7] We also see the Internet used extensively for lobbying and political campaigns.[8] More aggressively, some jurisdictions are experimenting with Internet voting. While the Arizona Democratic Party's use of the Internet during the 2000 U.S. presidential primary is perhaps the most visible example, governments in Brazil, Sweden, and Contra Costa County, California, have also run with online voting experiments.[9]

These and other digital democracy initiatives may eventually grow powerful. So far, however, work on the political and legislative side of governance (the "inputs") has been small relative to work on the executive side (the "outputs"). Given people's conservatism when it comes to political and constitutional structures—the devil you know is better than the one you do not—this should not be surprising. By changing our patterns of communication, the information age may eventually change how values are shaped and legitimated by our institutions of governance. So far, however, the initiatives to explore digital democracy have been cautious and gentle.

New Ways to Implement and Enforce Values: The Creation of Networked Government

How has information technology been used in policy implementation? Are computers being used in the delivery of government service, much as in the private sector? Not exactly. However, we do see that investments are following a similar path. The major steps have included

—using computer networks as a new channel for service delivery,

—beginning to reengineer services and create opportunities for self-service,

—expanding reliance on services outsourced to other agencies and the private sector,

—showing anxiety—but not much action yet—about social equity and cohesion, and

—beginning to contemplate the consequences of new forms of electronic money.

Each of these steps can be illustrated through examples.

Networked Service Delivery: Taking the Easy Next Steps

Government services have long been based on face-to-face interactions between citizens and bureaucrats. These interactions have fostered equal treatment and, when services have been simple, have allowed for manageable record keeping. As a result, however, most services offer little customization. Nonstandard problems often create nightmares for customers forced to travel to different facilities to get a building permit, resolve a tax dispute, or attend a public school class. Face-to-face, paper-based services have often proved burdensome to citizens and government workers alike.[10]

In recent years, such inefficiencies have become less tolerable. More citizens have jobs, and more families have two careers demanding attention.[11] The opportunity costs of waiting in line have increased. Many citizens have come to expect the convenience of network-delivered services. Once people learn that they can resolve a billing problem with a credit card from anywhere in the world and at any time of the day or night, they expect to solve problems in similar ways with local, state, or federal tax collectors.[12]

Fortunately, computers often provide ways to improve service accessibility, customization, and integration. Given the rapid expansion of interconnected networks, governments can offer convenience and other benefits through minor changes in organizational procedures. One of the most heavily used government websites, for example, allows citizens to download tax forms from the web; as the April 15 deadline for filing U.S. federal tax returns approaches, citizens find this to be of great value, especially on nights and weekends.[13]

Using computers for simple extensions of existing services has been a major focus for government technology initiatives.[14] Some examples include the accessible delivery service implemented by Ontario Business Connects, customized service delivery at the U.S. Occupational Safety and Health Administration, and government use of portals to provide integrated service delivery.

ACCESSIBLE SERVICE DELIVERY. As in most jurisdictions, businesses looking to locate in Ontario, Canada, have to find, understand, complete, and file numerous documents with multiple levels of government. Until recently, each of these tasks also had to be completed during regular working hours. Using the Ontario Business Connects (OBC) network, however, businesses can now file at their convenience, either online or at any number of convenient "single-window" locations.

Responding to an exodus of manufacturing firms in the mid-1990s, Ontario began searching for ways to improve the business climate. Ontario Business Connects represents the government's attempt to simplify and streamline business registration, renewal, and reporting, making it easier for businesses in Ontario to work with the government. Bringing together applications from various provincial agencies (the Ministry of Consumer and Business Services, the Ministry of Finance) and multiple levels of government (provincial, federal, and eventually municipal), OBC offers a single, integrated portal through which all the information and forms that businesses require can be found. In many cases, OBC allows businesses to complete their transactions twenty-four hours a day, seven days a week.

In addition to maintaining a web presence, OBC offers services through a number of other delivery channels. For example, OBC has established easy-to-use self-help workstations in locations such as shopping malls and public libraries. The organization also licenses "wholesalers" to package OBC services with other value-added services such as legal advice, accounting, and management consulting.

By making business-related processes available in more integrated ways, the government of Ontario has reduced the time required to complete business registration applications from three hours to thirty minutes. They have also eliminated the six- to eight-week mail-in waiting period by issuing information such as business name registrations instantly. Today more than 70 percent of business start-ups in Ontario use one of the OBC channels.[15]

CUSTOMIZED SERVICE DELIVERY. Like many sets of government regulations, those of the U.S. Occupational Safety and Health Administration (OSHA) are long and complicated and apply differently to different organizations under different circumstances. As a consequence, employers—and especially small businesses—struggle to understand which of OSHA's fourteen hundred pages of published regulations apply to them. Small businesses often overlook regulations or fail to document compliance appropriately.

To make compliance as easy as possible, OSHA's Regulatory Analysis Unit developed a series of software applications, which they call Expert Advisors. Functioning much like tax preparation software, OSHA Expert Advisors ask employers a series of questions about their businesses and the environments in which their employees work.[16] The software uses the answers to determine which regulations are relevant to a specific employer, presenting the employer with a customized report that not only outlines the relevant regulations but offers alternative courses of action to ensure compliance. The Expert Advisors not only save time for employers and OSHA compliance officers but also increase compliance levels, thus making work safer for employees.

The ultimate test for OSHA's Expert Advisors will be compliance efficiency and effectiveness. Although definitive measures are not yet available, the twelve Expert Advisors have been distributed free of charge and downloaded thousands of times, gaining a strongly positive reception among employers.

INTEGRATED SERVICE DELIVERY. As a gateway or single point of entry to government services, Internet portals have recently become extremely popular. Governments around the world are using portals to give their web presence a focal point, funneling citizens through a single site before directing them to information and services delivered by different departments.

Although portals as gateways can be valuable, portals can also do much more. Portals offer an opportunity to reorient services around the needs of citizens, enabling citizens to find information and services in intuitive and convenient ways. For example, rather than placing applications for marriage certificates under the Registry Division, citizens could find the application on a web page that integrates all marriage-related government services together.

Using many different strategies, government portals around the world have focused on integrating services in intuitive ways. Singapore's "e-Citizen" portal is organized around life events such as changing careers or retiring. Virginia launched "My Virginia" to allow citizens to personalize and control information as delivered. In Washington State citizens use a sophisticated search engine called "Ask George" that enables them to search all government websites at the same time, using plain language questions such as "How can I get a fishing permit?" The Canadian government's portal continuously updates a "Top Ten" list of services used by identifiable groups such as businesses and non-Canadians.[17]

As integrated service delivery continues to evolve, the latest trend is toward citizen relationship management. Citizen relationship management (CRM) conceives of government as a single entity rather than a series of departments, creating for the citizen a single and highly integrated experience with government. Through CRM, citizens can report a change of address with a single phone call rather than contacting multiple agencies. Privacy and security issues must be addressed before CRM gains widespread popularity; nevertheless, it is clear that governments will continue to take advantage of the improvements made possible through integrated service delivery.

Business registration and other services available when and where they are needed, expert systems to boost compliance with government regulations, and Internet portals—all are innovations designed to make services better through the use of networks. Such innovations are important, even though decidedly incremental. Furthermore, because networks can typically turn a staff-assisted transaction into one that can be handled by the citizen on a self-service basis, these and other innovations are likely to increase government efficiency more dramatically in the future. Note, however, that none of these innovations have either promised or achieved radical cost cutting. The benefits have been captured primarily as service accessibility, customization, and integration—and possibly as reduced demand on service employees—and not as tax cuts.

Reengineered Service and Self-service: Slow Progress

In the private sector, many technology-based changes have focused on reengineering. Reengineering does not seek incremental improvement—say, 10 percent—but aims instead at something much larger—say, 1,000 percent. The goals are radical, so the process is quite different from that used for normal productivity improvements.

Although reengineering has been pursued often in both the private and public sectors,[18] when public sector reengineering projects are examined closely, very few are found to involve radical change or cost cutting. What the public sector calls reengineering is generally a more gradual change than what is called for by the theory of reengineering. Let us look at two programs that have significantly—if not radically—changed how public sector work gets done: the San Diego Water Department and ServiceArizona.

ELIMINATING HAND-OFFS. For many tasks, specialists are more productive than generalists. However, dividing tasks among people and handing off work from one person to another often causes delays and other problems. Information technology can be extremely helpful in managing and coordinating such work flows. Computers operating on properly structured sets of rules can quickly look up guidance for the next step. Thus, the scope of work and the span of control for individual workers can be increased, reducing the need for workers to hand things back and forth.

The San Diego Water Department's use of hand-held technology is an example of how work can be simplified and improved. For years the department recorded all information related to the region's water infrastructure in detailed maps distributed to crews in huge, heavy books. Crews marked these maps to reflect changes that resulted from work being done and passed their changes to a central location for interpretation. The crews received updated maps every three to eighteen months. Not surprisingly, the errors and lags that resulted from data transcription created expensive and time-consuming problems for crews, who often found that their maps bore little resemblance to the real world. In 1998 the Water Department worked with the San Diego Data Processing Corporation to develop a computer-based infrastructure management system. The new system includes portable pen-based computers, complete with geographic positioning and geographic information systems. It both informs crew members about the infrastructure at a given facility and enables them to update the information directly. More important than the technology, however, is the change in work flow. Rather than scribbling notes on maps and passing them to a data entry center for interpretation, crews in the field now input the data themselves, uploading changes on a daily basis. This much more rapid data updating ensures that crews have accurate data when they leave for a job. It also redefines their jobs by making them responsible for the accuracy of the data.[19]

MOVING TO SELF-SERVICE. Improvements in efficiency through eliminating worker-to-worker hand-offs often pale in comparison with those possible through citizen self-service. Shifting tasks from government to citizens can often result in large savings to government and more convenient service to citizens.

Like the departments of motor vehicles in most states, the Arizona Motor Vehicle Division (MVD) is responsible for issuing licenses, registrations, and titles. The department handles 11 million transactions each year, and the number continues to grow as the population of Arizona expands. Faced with increasing transactions and limited resources, the Arizona MVD began looking for new ways to deliver service. Realizing that only 15 percent of their transactions required a state employee to validate the citizen's identity, the department turned to the idea of citizen self-service. Teaming with IBM, the Arizona MVD launched ServiceArizona in 1997 as one of the first state efforts to deliver MVD services online. ServiceArizona enables users to complete simple transactions, such as renewing a vehicle registration or ordering personalized license plates, all by themselves over the Internet.

In its first year, the 5 percent of Arizona residents who used ServiceArizona gave it a 99 percent positive satisfaction rating. Within two years, 13 percent of all annual registrations were completed through ServiceArizona. Moreover, the electronic self-service channel was 71 percent cheaper per transaction. Since it was first launched, ServiceArizona has expanded the number of services offered and has placed kiosks in MVD offices and other locations. Having highlighted the potential for self-service, ServiceArizona has provided leadership for other states to follow.[20]

Outsourcing: Much Smoke, Some Fire

Coordinating work through bureaucratic hierarchies typically economizes on information processing. By their nature, however, hierarchies operate many activities at a less than optimal scale. They also shield employees from market pressures for efficiency. Thus, if a given project (for example, developing a new software system) would be equally costly from an internal or an external unit, the production part of the cost would typically be higher for the internal approach. By the same logic, the coordination part of the cost (finding the right supplier, negotiating and monitoring contracts, and the like) would be higher for the external approach. Over time, as coordination costs fall more or less proportionately for both internal and external approaches, the external or market-based suppliers will grow relatively more attractive because they will enjoy bigger cost reductions. Market-based suppliers should also benefit as competition forces them to pay closer attention to customer needs and to innovation.[21]

This argument suggests that the information age will encourage new outsourcing in both the private and public sectors. Although government support for outsourcing has often been more rhetorical than real, in 2001 the U.S. Office of Management and Budget directed government agencies to open at least 5 percent of their jobs to competition in the next year and to set a target of holding 50 percent of all jobs open for competition.[22] In recent years, outsourcing has become less tactical (designed to cut costs or payroll) and more strategic (allowing government to focus on its core competencies—"steering"—while giving other organizations the work—the "rowing").[23] At the local level, for example, the County of San Diego has outsourced the management of all its information technology resources.[24] At the state level, governments such as North Carolina, Virginia, and Montana are hiring third-party organizations to build and manage their Internet portals, e-procurement systems, and other online applications. At the national level, U.S. electronic procurement systems are growing more like those of commercial enterprises,[25] and the United Kingdom is moving aggressively to outsource all data processing within Inland Revenue, its national tax collection agency.[26]

As the information age reduces coordination costs, look for continued government outsourcing. Although outsourcing will often be mistake ridden and controversial, it should—to the extent that it enhances competition—lead to better and more innovative services. It will also force a greater fraction of organizational life into the private sector, with potentially more stressful work lives for those pushed from public sector to private sector managerial environments.

Social Equity and Cohesion: Serious Anxiety
but Not Much Government Action

Many leaders believe that the information age will produce strong economic growth but only at the cost of growing inequality and divisiveness.[27] Clearly, in contrast with the first two-thirds of the twentieth century, recent decades have expanded the gap between rich and poor. This trend may continue, given that many jobs in the knowledge economy require expensive educational investments as a prerequisite. Climbing the ladder is now more difficult than ever because the skill sets required to reach the top are not easily acquired on the job.[28]

Inequality is a problem of ethics as well as politics, efficiency, and social stability. To reduce the number of information "have-nots" in an era of digital services, some governments are working toward a new definition of universal access. Others argue that government should do more to foster open standards and direct subsidies for computer-based services, especially for education and health. Typical proposals call for free access to electronic services through libraries, schools, and hospitals. Other proposals seek stronger intervention to protect those who would be harmed by globalization.[29]

On the opposite side of most equity issues, supporters of free markets argue that the government should not intervene strongly, at least not yet. They believe that government is not capable of sensible regulation or investment and that the best hope is to allow competitive markets to produce low unit costs; after all, unsubsidized television reaches more households than subsidized telephones.[30] In the grand scheme, income inequality results when some group is able to restrict access to a critical factor of production such as land or capital. In the information age, however, codified knowledge is the critical factor of production, and it may be easily replicated to flow freely throughout the world. Knowledge of job openings and of who is available to fill them may also become more efficiently networked, serving in the long run to increase rather than decrease equity.[31]

So far, the debates about equity have not had much impact on government action. Governments feel they are too poor to invest much.[32] Furthermore, given how easy it is for jobs in cyberspace to be moved from high-tax to low-tax jurisdictions, protecting equity by taxing Peter to pay Paul is not likely to become widespread or effective in the near future.

Electronic Money: A Force for New Pricing and Tax Policies?

In the ancient world, the development of coins and paper money facilitated trade. It is clearly easier for a shoemaker to use cash to buy a loaf of bread than to barter with the baker. Money and pricing systems thus support complexity in the organization of economic activity. In the information age, new payment methods based on computer networks—electronic money—may exert a similarly pervasive influence on how activities are priced and organized. Electronic money will make pricing and payments of small amounts (less than a penny, for example) efficient. In addition, electronic money should provide better security against fraudulent trading (through stronger encryption to authenticate messages and identities); it will also offer opportunities for anonymity (as happens today with cash).[33]

Electronic money may thus make it possible for governments to efficiently administer fees for new services or for services that are now given away free. Examples would include fees for the research and analysis of census data, for motor vehicle titles and owner histories, for surveyor reports, for property tax data, and for name and address services.

Governmental fees, of course, are controversial. The core argument is about who should pay for services—the users or the public in general. To the extent that the general public gains the benefits of use—as is true for most regulatory services—then broadly based taxes clearly make the most sense. To the extent, however, that the consumers directly capture the benefits—as for services such as campsite reservations—then fees make sense, as they do in the private sector. If there is a mix of beneficiaries—as when auto records are used both to ensure highway safety (a public benefit) and to improve car company profits through marketing—then perhaps the beneficiaries should pay proportionate to their benefits. The pricing system could serve to allocate joint costs in such cases.[34]

Pricing systems could also be constructed for transactions internal to the government. It is clear that government agencies do not share information easily with one another despite repeated exhortations to do so. Requests to freely provide data to outside agencies—even simple data such as names and addresses—are typically viewed by the recipients of such requests as unfunded mandates. However, once electronic money options are more fully implemented, it should become much easier to keep track of the producers and users of any piece of data. This would permit transaction prices even for things as minor as looking up a single name and address. With this kind of pricing, public organizations might be given better incentives to "share" the data they have collected and cleaned. In general, electronic money might create sizable information markets within and among government agencies and the public.

Although the use of electronic money might encourage marketlike activity, it might also encourage black-market or fraudulent activity (in which transactions are invisible to the government or payments are made to fraudulent parties). Cheap computing leads to powerful encryption and the ability of any two parties to keep secrets from the rest of society.[35] These secrets could include deposits and withdrawals at offshore banks. Electronic cash could make such secret trades easier, much as babysitter clubs, neighborhood-based service coupons, and cash payments today support activities that are rarely taxed. Invisible trades could conceivably grow into a meaningful threat to the tax base, especially for taxes based on the (easily moved) location of an income-generating activity instead of the (not so easily moved) residency of the receiver. Although large corporations may not be prime candidates for hiding transactions, individuals and small operations will be sorely tempted. Note also that fraud in electronic government payment systems—such as the earned income tax credit or Medicare and Medicaid payments—is also a threat. Electronic fraud has already grown to huge if largely invisible proportions.[36]

Changes in Governance: Just the Start of Something Big?

Governments are building huge and interconnected computer networks, but we have a long way to go before these become ubiquitously available to all workers and citizens. The momentum is clearly established, however, and nothing is likely to stop it. Putting services on these networks so they can be "virtually integrated"—that is, found and accessed by a few clicks of the mouse or, in a few years, by a few spoken words[37]—will continue until nearly all services offer network access as an option. That alone will significantly change the way people interact with government.

More fundamental reengineering will take longer. Nevertheless, given ongoing pressures to do so, and ongoing support for leading-edge practice through efforts such as the Clinton administration's National Partnership for Reinventing Government, governments will continue to pursue technology-related productivity and other innovations. Outsourcing will continue to expand. In addition, more governments will begin to work with the private sector to reform entire industries and economic infrastructures, much as

Table 9-1. *Impacts of the Information Age on Governance*

Future direction	Possible 2010 milestone
Shaping and legitimating values: nongeographic communities (the Internet) and digital democracy (new participation options)	—Fifteen hours per capita per week online, with greater involvement in and identification with nongeographic communities —15 percent of all purchasing online, with some online voting

Enforcing values: heavily networked and outsourced government
    —Reengineered processes, customization
    —Rich self-service options
    —User charges, transfer pricing
    —Collaborations on services, security, tax policies
	—95 percent penetration of net to all government workers
	—50 percent of government work outsourced
	—30 percent unit cost reduction of half of government services
	—20 percent of transactions on a self-service basis
	—20 percent of government revenues via user charges
	—Government-wide indexing and search engine standardization, security redundancies, and antifraud strategies

Core principle: adapting to new conditions and needs	Consensus needed on the imperative for research and development (not just DoD–based), with aggressive diffusion of best practice

Singapore has been doing for the past several decades.[38] Multinational and nongovernmental groups such as ICANN will be formed to govern different elements of cyberspace. Over the next ten to fifteen years, the expansion of network-based communications should exert a strong influence on how communities are formed and governed. Table 9-1 summarizes some of the predicted directions for governance and some milestones that may be reached by approximately 2010.[39]

So far, the impacts of the information age on government policymaking have been rather modest. We have been nibbling at digital democracy, little more. While net-enabled communication has begun to exert an influence on social values and politics, individuals and institutions have been slow to risk fundamental change. Politics and governance are about resolving conflicts, and efficiency is not the paramount virtue. Nevertheless, somewhat behind the scenes, initiatives such as ICANN and the open-source movement are promoting bigger proposals for change in how policies are made.[40] These and other proposals may grow extremely important as the proportion of human interactions conducted over computer networks increases.

The impacts of the information age on policy implementation and traditional governmental bureaucracies have been, in contrast, much clearer and more immediate. Public organizations are rapidly becoming networked, and they are using these networks to produce and deliver services. This will ultimately lead to efficiency improvements, much as has happened in the private sector.[41] Government bureaucracies will gradually become flatter, faster, and more customer friendly. Services will become better integrated and customized, with rich self-service options. Fees rather than taxes will be used more extensively to raise revenues and coordinate production and consumption.

As we proceed more deeply into the information age, the new core value and challenge for governance—at both organizational and societal levels— will be to learn how to adapt to new conditions and needs. To govern successfully, we must figure out how to protect public safety and prevent abuses of power while we simultaneously promote governmental flexibility and learning. We have made some progress on this problem, but our status as we enter the twenty-first century might best be described as "just at the start of something big."

Notes

1. For the importance of diversity and even irritation in responding to adaptive challenges, see Ronald A. Heifetz, *Leadership without Easy Answers* (Harvard University Press, 1994.)

2. An exploration of future governments and their possible specialization by function can be found in Bruce E. Tonn and David Feldman, "Non-spatial Government," *Futures,* vol. 27 (January–February 1995), p. 11, n. 1. Tonn and Feldman view information technology as a possible catalyst for government specialization by function, creating a nonspatial government populated by individuals with a strong affinity for one another but who do not necessarily share common spatial boundaries, another government that is spatial and responsible for infrastructure, and others with responsibility for enforcement and coordination. See also Robert Rotenberg and Gary McDonogh, *The Cultural Meaning of Urban*

Space (Westport, Conn.: Bergin and Garvey, 1993); Gerald E. Frug, "Geography of Community," *Stanford Law Review,* vol. 48, no. 5 (1996), pp. 1047–1108.

3. Limited experiments in exploring the practicality of direct decisionmaking when dealing with complex problems have been conducted in the United States. A report of one such effort can be found in Dick Sclove, "Telecommunications and the Future of Democracy: Preliminary Report on the First U.S. Citizens' Panel," *Loka Alert,* vol. 4, no. 3 (1997), Loka Institute (www.amherst.edu/~loka/alerts/loka.4.3.htm [June 2001]).

4. Alvin Toffler, *Creating a New Civilization* (Atlanta: Turner Publishing, 1995).

5. The ICANN website may be found at www.icann.org. See also NGO and Academic ICANN Study (NAIS), "The Public Voice, Legitimacy, and ICANN: An Interim Report," May 2001 (www.naisproject.org/report/interim [June 2001]); Steve Kettman, "ICANN Cannot, Say Critics," *Wired News,* June 9, 2001 (www.wired.com/news/politics/0,1283,44404,00.html [June 2001]); Steve Kettman, "ICANN Chief Strikes Back," *Wired News,* June 13, 2001 (www.wired.com/news/politics/0,1283,44480,00.html [June 2001]).

6. How information technologies are transforming citizen experience of the democratic process—and potentially the democratic process itself—is explored in Lawrence K. Grossman, *The Electronic Republic: Reshaping Democracy in the Information Age* (Penguin, 1996). More on the impact of technology on governance can be found in Frances Cairncross, "The Death of Distance," *Economist,* September 30, 1995, p. S5.

7. Pamela Varley with Ted Lascher, "Blip on the Screen or Wave of the Future? 'Electronic Democracy' in Santa Monica," teaching case 16-91-1031.0, John F. Kennedy School of Government, Harvard University, 1991. The case explores a "participatory democracy" experiment in southern California involving the establishment of a network of computer terminals to allow citizens to discuss public affairs online, both with one another and with elected officials. The case reviews the two years of the system's operation, including a description of the Public Electronic Network (PEN) system's apparent effect in influencing a new city policy on homelessness. The relatively small number of users, however, as well as the indifference of some elected officials to the system, raises questions about the extent of the impact of such a system and about whether technological innovation dramatically changes assumptions about the role of representative democracy.

8. See Elaine Ciulla Kamarck, "Campaigning on the Internet in the Elections of 1998," in Elaine Ciulla Kamarck and Joseph Nye Jr., eds., *Democracy.com? Governance in a Networked World* (Hollis, N.H.: Hollis Publishing, 1999); Lawrence K. Grossman, *The Electronic Republic* (London: Penguin Books, 1996); and Cairncross, "The Death of Distance." Also see Wayne Rash Jr., *Politics on the Nets: Wiring the Political Process* (New York: W. H. Freeman, 1997); Graeme Browning and Daniel J. Weitzner, *Electronic Democracy: Using the Internet to Influence American Politics* (Wilton, Conn.: Pemberton Press, 1996); W. Russell Neuman, Lee McKnight, and Richard Jay Solomon, *The Gordian Knot: Political Gridlock on the Information Highway* (MIT Press, 1996); Steven E. Miller, *Civilizing Cyberspace: Policy, Power, and the Information Superhighway* (New York: ACM Press, 1996); Roza Tsagarousianou, Damian Tambini, and Cathy Bryan, eds., *Cyberdemocracy, Technology, Cities, and Civic Networks* (Routledge, 1998); Jerome R. Ravetz, ed., *Cyberfutures: Culture and Politics on the Information Superhighway* (NYU Press, 1996); and Kevin A. Hill and John E. Hughes, *Cyberpolitics: Citizen Activism in the Age of the Internet (People, Passions, and Power)* (New York: Rowman and Littlefield, 1998).

9. California Internet Voting Task Force, "A Report on the Feasibility of Internet Voting," January 2000 (www.ss.ca.gov/executive/ivote [June 2001]); David Schwartz, "Arizona Makes E-voting History," *ZD Net News,* March 7, 2000 (www.zdnet.com/zdnn/ stories/news/0,4586,2457141,00.html [June 2001]); David Plotnikoff, "Internet Voting Gets a Trial Run," *Contra Costa (California) Times,* October 29, 2000 (www.contracostatimes. com/computing/columnists/plotnikoff/stories/029modem_20001029.htm [June 2001]); Joe Berkofsky, "Can the Swedes Swing the Net Vote?" *TechTV News,* April 11, 2001 (www.techtv.com/print/story/0,23102,3321412,00.html [June 2001]).

10. Jane Fountain, Linda Kaboolian, Steven Kelman, and Jerry Mechling, *Customer Service Excellence: Using Information Technologies to Improve Service Delivery in Government* (Strategic Computing and Telecommunications in the Public Sector Program, John F. Kennedy School of Government, Harvard University, 1994). See also Erin Research, *Citizens First 2000: Report on "Have Your Say!"—A Survey on Improving Government Services,* Institute of Public Administration of Canada, May 2001 (www.erinresearch.com [June 2001]); reports on customer service by the National Partnership for Reinventing Government, including *Putting Customers First '97: Standards for Serving the American People,* October 1997 (govinfo.library.unt.edu/npr/library/review.html [June 2001]).

11. According to Donald J. Hernandez, chief of the Marriage and Family Statistics Branch of the U.S. Bureau of the Census, "Between 1940 and 1989, the percentage of young children living in dual-earner families (that is, two-parent families with both parents in the labor force) increased sevenfold, from 5% to 38%. During the same period, the proportion of children living with a lone parent who worked increased fivefold, from 2% to 13%"; Donald J. Hernandez, "Changing Demographics: Past and Future Demands for Early Childhood Programs," *Future of Children,* vol. 5 (Winter 1995).

12. Jane Fountain, in a survey of toll-free telephone-center operators from the public and private sectors, has found that "callers to private sector over-the-telephone operations are generally more pleasant than those who use public sector over-the-telephone lines." A number of reasons are cited, including the generally more difficult nature of the calls; Jane Fountain, "The Use of 800 Numbers in Government," in Fountain and others, *Customer Service Excellence.* For more research on delivery channels, see Erin Research, *Citizens First 2000.*

13. Steven E. Brier, "Library/Tax-Filing Web Sites: It May Still Be Certain, but at Least It's Easier," *New York Times,* January 21, 1999, p. G8.

14. All examples that follow are taken from work by the Harvard Policy Group on Network-Enabled Services and Government (www.ksg.harvard.edu/stratcom/hpg) and the Innovations in American Government Program (www.ksg.harvard.edu/innovations).

15. The Ontario Business Connects website is at www.ccr.gov.on.ca/obc. Further details about OBC can be found in two case studies: "ONCE Corporation: Case Study, Ontario Business Connects," prepared for Lac Carling III Congress, Bromont, Quebec, June 17, 1999 (www.ipaciapc.ca/esd [June 2001]); and "ONCE Corporation: Establishing Ontario as the Preferred Jurisdiction for Business Formation and Growth, Ontario Business Connects," prepared for Lac Carling IV Congress, Manoir Saint Sauveur, Quebec, May 15–17, 2000 (www.ipaciapc.ca/esd[June 2001]).

16. The OSHA Expert Advisors can be found at www.osha-slc.gov/dts/osta/oshasoft/ osha-advisors.html.

17. Singapore's e-Citizen portal can be found at www.ecitizen.gov.sg. The "My Virginia" site can be linked from the main Virginia page at www.state.va.us. Washington State's "Ask

George" can be found at access.wa.gov. The Canadian government's dynamic "Top Ten" list of links can be found at businessgateway.ca.

18. Influential process-design literature includes Thomas H. Davenport, *Process Innovation: Reengineering Work through Information Technology* (Harvard Business School Press, 1993); Michael Hammer and James Champy, *Reengineering the Corporation: A Manifesto for Business Revolution* (New York: Harper Business, 1993); Michael Hammer, "Reengineering Work: Don't Automate, Obliterate," *Harvard Business Review* (July–August 1990), p. 104.

19. For more detail, see Ed Barker, "SWIMming in San Diego: Hand-held Computing and Enterprise Systems in the San Diego Water Department," teaching case study (unassigned), John F. Kennedy School of Government, Harvard University, 2000.

20. The ServiceArizona site can be found at www.servicearizona.com.

21. Lynda M. Applegate, F. Warren McFarlan, and James L. McKenney, *Corporate Information Systems Management,* 5th ed. (Boston: McGraw-Hill, 1999). Also see John F. Rockart and Christine V. Bullen, eds., *The Rise of Managerial Computing: The Best of the Center for Information Systems Research, Sloan School of Management, Massachusetts Institute of Technology* (Homewood, Ill.: Dow Jones-Irwin, 1986).

22. Office of Management and Budget, "Performance Goals and Management Initiatives for the FY 2002 Budget," memo M-01-15, March 9, 2001 (www.whitehouse. gov/omb/memoranda/m01-15.pdf [June 2001]).

23. David Osborne and Ted Gaebler, *Reinventing Government: How the Entrepreneurial Spirit Is Transforming the Public Sector* (New York: Plume Books, 1993).

24. Donna Young, "San Diego County Banks on Outsourcing," *Government Computer News: State and Local,* December 2000 (www.gcn.com/state/vol6_no12/snapshot/919-1.html [June 2001]).

25. Using the U.S. General Services Administration (GSA) Advantage (www.gsaadvantage.gov), federal employees can purchase goods and services quickly from a central location. The FedBizOpps site (www.fedbizopps.gov) serves as a central site for government employees to post government-wide procurement opportunities. The U.S. federal government is exploring the use of reverse auctions with Buyers.Gov (www.buyers.gov).

26. John Grigsby, "Outsourcing: Taxing Spectre of Big Brother Public Sector Policy under Labour Is Changing," *Daily Telegraph* (London), May 28, 1997, p. 9; Michael Dempsey, "Suppliers Are Cautious—Outsourced Services: Despite the Lucrative Contracts Available, Some IT Companies Are Wary about Taking on Too Much Government Work as the Switch to Outsourcing Continues," *Financial Times* (London), November 5, 1998, p. 19. Inland Revenue's home page is www.inlandrevenue.gov.uk/home.htm.

27. Canadian government officials have explored the future of the information age through the use of scenario planning, similar to that used by Royal Dutch Shell. Four primary possible outcomes emerged from their effort, including an economy both rich and socially cohesive, one rich but not socially cohesive, one neither rich nor socially cohesive, and one socially cohesive but not rich; Steven A. Rosell et al., *Changing Maps: Governing in a World of Rapid Change* (Ottawa: Carleton University Press, 1995). Surveys of the perceptions of leaders in government have also been conducted by Harvard's Program on Strategic Computing and Telecommunications in the Public Sector, in which respondents describe their organizations as "lagging far behind the private sector in using [information technol-

ogy] for fundamental improvements in organizational strategies or operations"; Jerry Mechling and Thomas M. Fletcher, *Information Technology and Government: The Need for New Leadership* (Strategic Computing and Telecommunications in the Public Sector Program, John F. Kennedy School of Government, Harvard University, 1996), p. 33.

28. Robert B. Reich, *The Work of Nations: Preparing Ourselves for Twenty-first-Century Capitalism* (Knopf, 1991).

29. Gary Chapman, "High-Tech Heroes Who Work for the Public Good," *Los Angeles Times,* October 26, 1998. Gary Chapman, "Time to Cast Aside Political Apathy in Favor of Creating a New Vision for America," *Los Angeles Times,* August 19, 1996 (www.utexas.edu/lbj/21cp/Convention.html [June 2001]. For proposals similar to those calling for free access, see the initiatives of Vice President Al Gore's National Partnership for Reinventing Government (govinfo.library.unt.edu/npr/default.html), particularly its *Access America* program and report (govinfo.library.unt.edu/npr/library/announc/access/acessrpt.html [June 2001]). Patrick J. Buchanan, *The Great Betrayal: How American Sovereignty and Social Justice Are Being Sacrificed to the Gods of the Global Economy* (Little, Brown, 1998).

30. Neuman, McKnight, and Solomon, *The Gordian Knot.* The authors make the argument for a historical pattern of innovations "freezing" into Gordian knots under the pressure of social, political, and business forces brought about by new technologies. The emergence of each new technology brought about a clash of economic superpowers struggling to control access, standards, and proprietary technology in a given emerging industry.

31. Note that the One-Stop Career Centers of the Department of Labor have created a dramatic shift toward self-service that also seem to promote equity. In the early 1990s, 95 percent or more of the transactions in government employment centers were staff mediated. By 1998, however, nearly 80 percent of the transactions occurred through the Internet or in computer-based resource rooms. Because of the Internet base for service delivery, libraries and even church social rooms have become nearly full-service career centers. Electronic government service delivery has the potential to equalize access to key information that was once available primarily to those of high status with valuable and inherently exclusionary networks of personal connections.

32. National Research Council, National Information Infrastructure Steering Committee, *Unpredictable Certainty: Information Infrastructure through 2000* (Washington, 1996).

33. Stephen J. Kobrin, "Electronic Cash and the End of National Markets," *Foreign Policy,* vol. 107 (June 1, 1997), pp. 65–77.

34. Jerry Mechling and Victoria Sweeney, *Finding and Funding Good IT Initiatives in Government* (Sacramento: Government Technology Press, 1998); Kevin McCarthy, J. K. Neels, C. P. Rydell, J. P. Stucker, and A. H. Pascal, "Exploring Benefit-Based Finance for Local Government Services: Must User Charges Harm the Disadvantaged?" (Santa Monica, Calif.: RAND Corporation, 1984).

35. Jean Camp, *Trust and Risk in Internet Commerce* (MIT Press, 2000). For more information on encryption, see Electronic Privacy Information Center (www.epic.org); Electronic Frontier Foundation (www.eff.org); Internet Free Expression Alliance (www.ifea.net); Global Internet Liberty Campaign (www.gilc.org); Harvard's Information Infrastructure Project (www.ksg.harvard.edu/iip); and Harvard's Berkman Center for Law and Society (cyber.law.harvard.edu/).

36. This enormous social problem is well documented in Malcolm K. Sparrow, *License to Steal: Why Fraud Plagues America's Health Care System* (Boulder: Westview Press, 1996).

37. Bob Weinstein, "Now You Can Be on Speaking Terms with Your Computer," *Boston Globe,* November 5, 1998, p. F2.

38. See Harvard Business School teaching case series on Singapore's efforts, including Benn Konsynski and John King, "Singapore TradeNet: A Tale of One City," teaching case 9-191-009, Harvard Business School, Harvard University, 1995; Lynda M. Applegate, Boon-Siong Neo, and John King, "Singapore TradeNet: The Tale Continues," teaching case 9-193-136, Harvard Business School, Harvard University, 1995; and Lynda M. Applegate, Boon-Siong Neo, and John King, "Singapore TradeNet: Beyond TradeNet to the Intelligent Island," teaching case 9-196-105, Harvard Business School, Harvard University, 1995.

39. Although the numbers in table 9-1 could all be estimated through sampling from field observations and other data, the figures used in this paper were based on intuitive judgments ("guesstimates," not estimates). Getting better numbers would make an interesting and useful measurement project.

40. See Larry Lessig, *Code and Other Laws of Cyberspace* (Basic Books, 1999).

41. According to Eric Brynjolfsson and Shinkyu Yang, the pendulum is currently swinging away from the view of the skeptics such as Robert Solow—"You can see the computer age everywhere but in the productivity statistics" (quoted in Erik Brynjolfsson, "The Productivity Paradox of Information Technology," *Communications of the ACM,* vol. 36 [1993], p. 66)—to the views expressed in a number of *Fortune* magazine articles regarding the "technology payoff" (including Stratford Sherman, "How to Bolster the Bottom Line: Information Technology Special Report," *Fortune,* vol. 128 [Autumn 1993], p. 14). The truth, it appears, probably lies somewhere in between. For an in-depth examination of literature on the "productivity paradox," see Brynjolfsson and Yang, "Information Technology and Productivity: A Review of the Literature," *Advances in Computers,* vol. 43 (1996), pp. 179–214.

10 ROBERT O. KEOHANE
JOSEPH S. NYE JR.

Power and Interdependence
in the Information Age

THROUGHOUT THE TWENTIETH CENTURY, modernists proclaimed that technological change would dramatically transform world politics. In 1910 Norman Angell declared wars to be irrational as a result of economic interdependence, and he looked forward to the day when they would therefore be obsolete.[1] Modernists in the 1970s saw telecommunications and jet travel as creating a "global village" and believed that the territorial state, which has been dominant in world politics for the four centuries since feudal times ended, was being eclipsed by nonterritorial actors such as multinational corporations, transnational social movements, and international organizations. Similarly, prophets such as Peter Drucker, Alvin and Heidi Toffler, and Esther Dyson claim that the contemporary information revolution is bringing an end to the hierarchical bureaucratic organization, or is creating the "disintermediation of government," leading to a new electronic feudalism with overlapping communities and jurisdictions laying claim to multiple layers of citizens' identities and loyalties.

The modernists of past generations were partly right. Angell's understanding of the impact of war on interdependence was insightful: World War I wrought unprecedented destruction, not only on the battlefield but also in society by wrecking the sociopolitical systems and networks of economic interdependence that had thrived during the relatively peaceful years since 1815. As the modernists of the 1970s predicted, multinational corporations, nongovernmental organizations, and global financial markets have indeed become immensely more significant during the past quarter century. The state, however, has been more resilient than modernists have expected. Not only do states continue to command the loyalties of a vast majority of the world's people; their control over material resources in most wealthy countries of the Organization for Economic Cooperation and Development, where markets are so important, has stayed at a third to one-half of gross domestic product.

The modernists of 1910 and the 1970s were right about the direction of change but simplistic about its consequences. Like some contemporary commentators on the information revolution, they moved too directly from technology to political consequences, without sufficiently considering the continuity of belief systems, the persistence of institutions, or the strategic options available to leaders of states. They failed to analyze the extent to which holders of power could wield that power to shape or distort patterns of societal interdependence.

More than twenty years ago in our book *Power and Interdependence,* we analyzed the politics of such transnational issues as trade, monetary relations, and oceans policy. We commented then that

> modernists point correctly to the fundamental changes now taking place, but they often assume without sufficient analysis that advances in technology and increases in social and economic transactions will lead to a new world in which states, and their control of force, will no longer be important. Traditionalists are adept at showing flaws in the modernist vision by pointing out how military interdependence continues, but find it very difficult accurately to interpret today's multidimensional economic, social, and ecological interdependence.[2]

This is still true for the information age.

Interdependence is not new. What is new is the virtual erasing of the costs of distance as a result of the information revolution—sometimes called globalization. No longer is it sufficient to analyze flows of raw materials, goods, and capital across borders or to understand how states construct territorial boundaries on the high seas. Cyberspace is itself a "place": everywhere and nowhere. Traditionally, political activity has focused first at the local level, extending to national and international spheres only as the activity being regulated escaped jurisdictional boundaries. The contemporary information revolution, however, is inherently global, since "cyber-place" is divided on a nongeographic basis. The address extensions "edu," "org," and "com" are not geographic.

Prophets of a new cyberworld, however, like modernists before them, often overlook the extent to which the new world overlaps and depends upon the traditional world in which power depends upon geographically based institutions. In 1998, 100 million people used the Internet. Even if this number reaches 1 billion in 2005, as some experts predict, a large portion of the world's people will not be participating. Moreover, globalization is far from universal. Three-quarters of the world's population does not own a telephone, much less a modem and a computer. Rules will be necessary to govern cyberspace—not only to protect lawful users from criminals but also to ensure intellectual property rights. Rules require authority, whether in the form of public government or private or community governance. Classic issues of politics—who governs, on what terms, who benefits—are as relevant to cyberspace as to traditional physical space.

Information is power, as Francis Bacon wrote four hundred years ago. Undoubtedly, the information revolution has profound political implications. It therefore makes sense to seek to analyze some of these implications, using tools developed in studying the politics of interdependence. As traditionalist realists maintain, much will be the same: states will play important roles; vulnerability will lead to bargaining weakness, and lack of vulnerability to power; actors will seek to manipulate cyberspace, as they manipulate flows across borders, to enhance their power. Yet as modernists insist, the information revolution is not "déjà vu all over again." Cyberspace is truly global; it is harder to stop or even monitor the flow of information-carrying electrons than to do so for raw materials or goods; and dramatic reductions in the cost of information transmission make other resources relatively scarce.

In 1977 we raised the following question: what are the major features of world politics when interdependence, particularly economic interdependence, is extensive? One aspect of our analysis took the interstate system as given and asked how interstate power relations would be affected by economic interdependence, especially by vulnerabilities produced by such interdependence. The second dimension of our work went further, asking about the character of politics in domains in which conventional realist assumptions about international relations no longer applied. These thoughts led us to imagine a politics we called complex interdependence with three conditions: a minor role of military force, absence of hierarchy among issues, and multiple channels of contact among societies.

Conditions approximating complex interdependence were emerging even in the mid-1970s among wealthy democratic states. They affected both interstate relations and the emerging domain of transnational relations, in which nonstate actors played a major role. Yet there remained great variation among regions and across issues. Force was of minor significance in the relations between the United States and Canada or among the states of the European Union. But force remained of crucial significance in the U.S.-Soviet relationship or—as it still does—among many states in the Middle East, Africa, or Asia.

In this chapter we apply the same analytic lens to the contemporary information revolution. We analyze different types of information and how the information revolution has altered patterns of complex interdependence and address the impact of the information revolution on power among states. Finally, we explore some more novel implications of the information revolution for world politics. In particular, we argue that by drastically reducing the costs of transmitting information, the information revolution creates a new politics of credibility in which transparency will increasingly be a power asset.

The Information Revolution and Complex Interdependence

We use the term *information revolution* to refer to the rapid technological advances in computers, communications, and software that have led to dramatic decreases in the cost of processing and transmitting information. The price of a new computer has dropped by 19 percent a year since 1954, and information technologies have risen from 7 to nearly 50 percent of new investment. Computing power has doubled every eighteen months for the past thirty years; it now costs less than 1 percent of what it did in the early 1970s. Similarly, growth of the Internet and the World Wide Web has been exponential. Traffic on the Internet has been doubling every hundred days. The web was only invented in 1990. Communications bandwidths are expanding rapidly, and communications costs continue to fall. As late as 1980, phone calls over copper wire could carry one page of information a second; today a thin strand of optical fiber can transmit ninety thousand volumes in a second. As with steam at the end of the eighteenth century and electricity at the end of the nineteenth, there have been lags in productivity growth as society learns to utilize the new technologies. Although many industries and firms have been undergoing rapid structural changes since the 1980s, the economic transformation is far from complete. It is generally agreed that we are still in the early stages of the information revolution.

For our purposes, the distinguishing mark of the information revolution is the enormous reduction in the cost of transmitting information. For all practical purposes, the actual transmission costs have become negligible; hence the amount of information that can be transmitted is effectively infinite—as the proliferation of "spam" junk mail on the Internet suggests. Furthermore, neither costs nor the time taken to transmit messages are significantly related to distance. An Internet message to a colleague a few miles away may be routed through thousands of miles of computer networks; but neither the sender nor the recipient knows or cares.

However, the information revolution has not transformed world politics to a new politics of complete complex interdependence. One reason is that information does not flow in a vacuum; rather, it moves through political space that is already occupied. States have for the past four centuries established the political structure within which information flows across borders and other transactions take place.

The information revolution itself can be understood only within the context of the globalization of the world economy, which itself was deliberately fostered by U.S. policy, and by international institutions, for half a century after the end of World War II. In the late 1940s the United States sought to create an open international economy to forestall another depression and to contain communism. The resulting international institutions, formed on the basis of multilateral principles, fostered an environment that put a premium on markets and information. American-led market-based approaches have shaped developments in the technologies of transportation and communications. In turn, the information technologies and institutions have made it increasingly costly for states to turn away from the patterns of interdependence that had been created.

The information revolution occurred not merely within a preexisting political context but within one characterized by continuing military tensions and conflicts. Although the end of the cold war removed one set of military-related tensions, it left some in place (as in the Middle East) and created situations of state breaking and state making in which violence was used ruthlessly to attain political ends—notably in Africa, the Caucasus, central Asia, and southeastern Europe. Even in East Asia, the scene until recently of rapid economic growth, political-military rivalries persist. At the same time, the military presence of the United States plays a clearly stabilizing role in East Asia, central Europe, and—tenuously—in Bosnia. Contrary to some early predictions after the end of the cold war, the North Atlantic Treaty Organization remains popular in western and central Europe. Markets thrive only with secure property rights, which depend on a political framework—which in turn requires military security. To ignore the role of military security in an era of economic and information growth is like forgetting the importance of oxygen to our breathing.

Outside the democratic zone of peace, the world of states is not a world of complex interdependence: in many areas, realist assumptions about the role of military force and the dominance of security issues remain valid. However, the third feature of complex interdependence—multiple channels of contact among societies—has changed dramatically. We see an order-of-magnitude shift as a result of the information revolution. Now anyone with a computer can be a desktop publisher, and anyone with a modem can communicate with distant parts of the globe at trivial costs. Barriers to entry into the world "information market" have been dramatically lowered.

Earlier transnational flows were heavily controlled by large bureaucratic organizations, such as multinational corporations or the Catholic Church, with the resources to establish communication infrastructure. Such organizations remain important, but the vast cheapening of information transmission has now opened the field to loosely structured network organizations and even individuals. These nongovernmental organizations and networks are particularly effective in penetrating states without regard to borders and using domestic constituencies to set the agendas of national leaders. By vastly increasing the number of channels of contact among societies, the information revolution is changing the extent to which some aspects of world politics are approximating our notion of complex interdependence.

However, information is not like goods or pollution, for which quantities flowing across borders are meaningful. The quantity of information available in cyberspace means little by itself. To focus only on the quantity of information, and on attention to that information, would be to overlook the issue of information quality and distinctions among types of information. Information does not just exist; it is created. We therefore need to pay attention, as economists do, to incentives to create information. When we do so, we discover three different types of information that are sources of power in world politics.

Free information is information that actors are willing to create and send without financial compensation from the recipient. The sender gets advantages from the receiver's believing the information and hence has incentives to produce it. Motives may vary. Scientific information falls into the category of a public good, but persuasive messages, such as those in which politicians specialize, are more self-serving. Marketing, broadcasting, and propaganda are all examples of free information. The reduction in average costs of production and transmission has reduced barriers to entry and greatly increased the flows of free information. The explosion in the quantity of free information is perhaps the most dramatic effect of the information revolution.

Commercial information is information that actors are willing to create and send at a price. Actors neither gain nor lose by others' believing in the information, apart from the compensation they receive. For such information to be available on the Internet, issues of property rights must be resolved, so that producers of information can be compensated for its use. Creating commercial information before one's competitors can—if there is an effective system to protect intellectual property rights—generates first-mover advantages and enormous profits, as the history of Microsoft demonstrates. In contrast to free information, for which low average costs have had a strong impact on increasing flows, much of the profit from commercial information comes from the advantage of being first and the ability to withhold information unless recipients pay for it. The rapid growth of electronic commerce and the increase in global competition will be other important effects of the information revolution.

Strategic information is information that confers great advantage on actors only if their competitors do not possess it. Strategic information provides asymmetrical knowledge of a competitor's strategy so that the outcome of a game is altered. There is nothing new about strategic information: it is as old as espionage. One of the enormous advantages possessed by the United States in World War II was not only that it had broken Japan's codes but that it had done so without Japan's knowledge. In many cases, the quantity of strategic information may not be particularly important. For example, the strategic information available to the United States about the weapons programs of North Korea, Pakistan, or Iraq depends more on having reliable satellites or spies than on the vast flows of the Internet. Critical messages may be brief and delivered by dedicated communications systems.

In a nutshell, creators of free information benefit from others' believing in the information they possess. Creators of commercial information benefit if they are compensated. Creators of strategic information benefit most if their possession of the information is not known to others.

The information revolution alters patterns of complex interdependence by exponentially increasing the number of channels of communication in world politics—among individuals in networks, not just among individuals within bureaucracies. It appears, however, within the context of an existing political structure, and its effects on the flows of different types of information are highly variable. Free information will flow faster in the absence of regulation. Strategic information will be protected as much as possible—for example, by encryption technologies. The flow of commercial information will depend on whether effective rules that protect property rights in cyberspace are established—by governments, business, or nongovernmental organizations. Politics will affect the direction of the information revolution as much as it will be affected by it.

Information and Power among States

Knowledge is power: but what is power? A basic distinction is between behavioral power—the ability to obtain desired outcomes—and resource power—the possession of the resources that are usually associated with the ability to get the outcomes you want. Behavioral power, in turn, can be divided into hard and soft power. Hard power is the ability to get others to do what they otherwise would not do through threat of punishment or promise of reward. Whether by economic carrots or military sticks, the ability to coax or coerce has long been the central element of power. As we pointed out two decades ago, asymmetrical interdependence is an important source of hard power. The ability of the less vulnerable to manipulate or escape the constraints of an interdependent relationship at low cost is an important source of power. For example, in 1971 the United States increased its influence over the international monetary system by halting the convertibility of dollars into gold. In 1973 Arab states temporarily gained power from an oil embargo.

Soft power, on the other hand, is the ability to get desired outcomes because others want what an actor wants rather than do what an actor makes them do. It is the ability to achieve desired outcomes through attraction rather than coercion. It works by convincing others to follow or getting them to agree to norms and institutions that produce the desired behavior. Soft power can rest on the appeal of one's ideas or culture or the ability to set the agenda through standards and institutions that shape the preferences of others. It is the ability to frame issues. It depends largely on the persuasiveness of the free information that an actor seeks to transmit. If a state can make its power legitimate in the perception of others and establish international institutions that encourage others to define their interests in compatible ways, it may not need to expend as many of its costly traditional economic or military resources.

Hard and soft power are related, but they are not the same. Samuel P. Huntington is correct when he says that material success makes a culture and ideology attractive, and decreases in economic and military success lead to self-doubt and crises of identity. He is wrong, however, when he argues that soft power is power only when it rests on a foundation of hard power. The soft power of the Vatican did not wane because the size of the papal states diminished. Canada, Sweden, and the Netherlands tend to have more influence than some other states with equivalent economic or military capability. The Soviet Union had considerable soft power in Europe after World War II but squandered it with the invasions of Hungary and Czechoslovakia even at a time when Soviet economic and military power were still continuing to grow. Soft power varies over time and different domains. America's popular culture, with its libertarian and egalitarian currents, dominates film, television, and electronic communications in the world today. However, not all aspects of that culture are attractive to all others—for example, conservative Moslems. In that domain, American soft power is limited. Nonetheless, the spread of information and American popular culture has generally increased global awareness of and openness to American ideas and values. To some extent this reflects deliberate policies, but more often soft power is an inadvertent by-product.

The information revolution is also affecting power measured in terms of resources rather than behavior. In the eighteenth century, the European balance of power, territory, population, and agriculture provided the basis for infantry, which was a crucial power resource, and France was a principal beneficiary. In the nineteenth century, industrial capacity provided the crucial resources that enabled Britain and, later, Germany to gain dominance. By the mid-twentieth century, science, and particularly nuclear physics, contributed crucial power resources to the United States and the Soviet Union. In the twenty-first century, information technology broadly defined is likely to be the most crucial power resource.

The new conventional wisdom is that the information revolution has a decentralizing and leveling effect. As it reduces costs, economies of scale, and barriers of entry to markets, it should reduce the power of large states and enhance the power of small states and nonstate actors. In practice, however, international relations are more complex than the technological determinism of the new conventional wisdom suggests. Some aspects of the information revolution help the small; but some help the already large and powerful. There are several reasons for this.

First, important barriers to entry and economies of scale remain in some aspects of power that are related to information. For example, soft power is strongly affected by the cultural content of what is broadcast or appears in movies and television programs. Large established entertainment industries often enjoy considerable economies of scale in content production and distribution. The dominant American market share in films and television programs in world markets is a case in point.

Second, although it is now cheap to disseminate existing information, the collection and production of new information often requires major costly investments. In many competitive situations, it is the newness of information at the margin that counts more than the average cost of all information. Intelligence collection is a good example. States like the United States, Britain, and France have capabilities for collection and production that dwarf those of other nations. In some commercial situations, a fast follower can do better than a first mover, but in terms of power among states, to be a successful first mover is usually preferred.

Third, first movers are often the creators of the standards and architecture of information systems. The path-dependent development of such systems reflects the advantage of the first mover. The use of the English language and the pattern of top-level domain names on the Internet is a case in point. Partly because of the transformation of the American economy in the 1980s (which was missed or misunderstood by the prophets of decline) and partly because of large investments driven by the cold-war military competition, the United States was often the first mover and still enjoys a lead in the application of a wide variety of information technologies.

Fourth, military power remains important in some critical domains of international relations. Information technology has some effects on the use of force that benefit the small and some that favor the already powerful. The off-the-shelf commercial availability of what used to be costly military technologies benefits small states and nonstate actors and increases the vulnerability of large states. Information systems add lucrative targets for terrorist (including state-sponsored) groups. Other trends, however, strengthen the already powerful. Many military analysts refer to a revolution in military affairs that has been produced by the application of information technology. Space-based sensors, direct broadcasting, high-speed computers, and complex software provide the ability to gather, sort, process, transfer, and disseminate information about highly complex events that occur in wide geographic areas. This dominant battle-space awareness combined with precision force provides a powerful advantage. As the Persian Gulf war showed, traditional assessments of balances of weapons platforms such as tanks or planes become irrelevant unless they include the ability to integrate information with those weapons. Many of the relevant technologies are available in commercial markets, and weaker states can be expected to have many of them. The key, however, will be not the possession of fancy hardware or advanced systems but the ability to integrate a system of systems. In this dimension, the United States is likely to keep its lead, and in terms of information warfare, a small edge makes all the difference. For instance, a recent Australian assessment of the future balance of power in East Asia finds that the revolution in military affairs will not diminish and may, in some instances, even increase the American lead.

Contrary to the expectations of some theorists, the information revolution has not greatly decentralized or equalized power among states. If anything, thus far it has had the opposite effect. But what about reducing the role of governments and the power of all states? Here the changes are more likely to be along the lines the modernists predicted. To understand these changes, however, it is necessary first to explore how the information revolution, by minimizing the costs of transmitting information, has increased the relative significance of the scarce resource of attention and the implications of this shift for what we call the politics of credibility.

The Paradox of Plenty and the Politics of Credibility

To understand the effect of free information on power, one must first understand the paradox of plenty. A plenitude of information leads to a poverty of attention. Attention becomes the scarce resource, and those who can distinguish valuable signals from white noise gain power. Editors, filters, and cue givers become more in demand, and this is a source of power. There will be an imperfect market for evaluators. Brand names and the ability to bestow an international "Good Housekeeping Seal of Approval" will become more important.

Power, however, does not necessarily flow to those who can withhold information. Under some circumstances private information can cripple the credibility of those who have it. For instance, economists point out that sellers of used cars have more knowledge about their defects than potential buyers. Moreover, owners of bad cars are more likely to sell than owners of good ones. These facts lead potential buyers to discount the price they are willing to pay in order to adjust for unknown defects. Hence the result of the superior information of sellers is not to improve the average price they receive but instead to make them unable to sell good used cars for their real value. Unlike asymmetrical interdependence in trade, by which power goes to those who can afford to hold back or break trade ties, information power flows to those who can edit and credibly validate information to sort out what is both correct and important.

Hence among editors and cue givers, credibility is the crucial resource, and asymmetrical credibility is a key source of power. Reputation has always mattered in world politics, and it becomes even more important because of the paradox of plenty. The low cost of transmitting data means that the ability to transmit it is much less important as a power resource than it used to be, but the ability to filter information is more so. Political struggles focus less on control over the ability to transmit information than over the creation and destruction of credibility.

Three types of state action illustrate the value of credibility. Much of the traditional conduct of foreign policy occurs through the exchange of promises, which are valuable only insofar as they are credible. Hence, governments that can credibly assure potential partners that they will not act opportunistically will gain advantages over competitors whose promises are less credible. Second, to borrow from capital markets at competitive interest rates increasingly requires credible information about one's own financial situation. Finally, the exercise of soft power implies credibility in order to be persuasive.

One implication of the abundance of free information sources, and the role of credibility, is that soft power is likely to become less a function simply of material resources than in the past. When ability to produce and disseminate information is the scarce resource, limiting factors include the control of printing presses, radio stations, and newsprint. Hard power—for instance, using force to take over the radio station—can generate soft power. In the case of worldwide television, wealth can also lead to soft power. For instance, CNN was based in Atlanta rather than Amman or Cairo because of America's leading position in the industry and technology.

When Iraq invaded Kuwait in 1990, the fact that CNN was basically an American company helped to frame the issue, worldwide, as aggression (analogous to Hitler's actions in the 1930s) rather than as a justified attempt to reverse colonial humiliation (analogous to India's capture of Goa).

This close connection between hard and soft power is likely to be somewhat weakened under conditions of complex interdependence in an information age. Propaganda as a form of free information is not new. Adolf Hitler and Joseph Stalin used it effectively in the 1930s. Slobodan Milosevic's control of television was crucial to his power in Serbia. In Moscow in 1993 a battle for power was fought at a television station. In Rwanda, Hutu-controlled radio stations contributed to genocide. The power of broadcasting persists, but in years to come it will be increasingly supplemented by the Internet, with its multiple channels of communication controlled by multiple actors who cannot use force to control one another. The issue is not only which actors own television networks, radio stations, or websites—once a plethora of such sources exist—but who pays attention to which fountains of information and misinformation.

Soft power today can also be the legacy of yesterday's hard and soft power. Britain's resources more than a half century ago enabled it to construct the British Broadcasting Corporation (BBC), and the nature of British society and politics made the BBC what is has become: a relatively reliable and unbiased source of information worldwide. For Britain, as a result of the credibility it had established earlier, the BBC was an important soft-power resource in eastern Europe during the cold war. Now it has more competitors, but to the extent that it maintains credibility in an era of white noise, its value as a power resource may actually increase.

Broadcasting is a type of free information dispersal system that has long had an impact on public opinion. By focusing on some conflicts and human rights problems, broadcasters have pressed politicians to respond to some foreign conflicts rather than others—for example, Somalia rather than southern Sudan. Not surprisingly, governments have sought to influence, manipulate, or control television and radio stations—and have been able to do so with considerable success—because a relatively small number of physically located broadcasting sites have been used to reach many people with the same message. However, the shift from broadcasting to narrowcasting has major political implications. Cable television and the Internet enable senders to segment and target audiences. Even more important for politics is the interactive role of the Internet; it not only focuses attention but also facilitates coordination of action across borders.

Interactivity at low cost allows for the development of new virtual communities—people who imagine themselves as part of a single group regardless of how far apart they are physically from one another.

These technologies create new opportunities for nongovernmental actors. Advocacy networks find their potential impact vastly expanded by the information revolution, because the fax machine and the Internet enable them to send messages from the most obscure corners of the world, from the rain forests of Brazil or the villages of Chiapas or sweatshops in Southeast Asia. The movement that produced the recent landmine treaty was a coalition of network organizations working with middle-power governments like Canada, some individual politicians like Senator Patrick Leahy, and celebrities like Princess Diana to capture attention, set the agenda, and put pressure on political leaders. The role of nongovernmental organizations was also important as a channel of communication across delegations in the global warming discussions at Kyoto. Environmental groups and industry competed in Kyoto for the attention of the media from major countries, basing their arguments in part on the findings of nongovernmental scientists. Many observers have heralded a new era for nongovernmental organizations as a result of the information revolution; and there seems little doubt that substantial opportunities exist for a flowering of issue advocacy networks and virtual communities.

Yet the credibility of these networks is fragile. Greenpeace, for instance, imposed large costs on Royal Dutch Shell by criticizing Shell's planned disposal of its Brentspar drilling rig in the North Sea, but Greenpeace itself lost credibility and membership when it later had to admit the inaccuracy of some of its factual claims. The findings of atmospheric scientists about climate change have gained credibility, not just from the prestige of science but from the procedures developed in the Intergovernmental Panel on Climate Change for extensive and careful peer review of scientific papers and intergovernmental vetting of executive summaries. The climate organization is an example of an intergovernmental information-legitimating institution whose major function is to give coherence and credibility to masses of scientific information about climate change.

As the Intergovernmental Panel on Climate Change example shows, the importance of credibility is giving increasing importance to transnational networks of like-minded experts. By framing issues in which knowledge is an important factor, such professional communities become important actors in forming coalitions and in bargaining processes. By creating knowledge, they can provide the basis for effective cooperation. To be effective, however, the procedures by which this information is produced have to appear unbiased. It is increasingly recognized that scientific information is in part socially constructed. To be credible, the information has to be produced through a process that is dominated by professional norms and appears transparent and procedurally fair. Even if their information is credible, professional communities will not resolve contentious issues that involve major distributional costs. They will, however, become more significant actors in the politics of decisionmaking.

The politics of soft power does not depend only on the information shapers, who seek to persuade others to adopt their practices and values. It also depends on the characteristics of their targets: the information takers, or the targets of free information flows. Of course, the shapers and takers are often the same people, organizations, or countries in different capacities. Information shapers, as we have seen, require credibility. The takers, on the other hand, will be differentially receptive depending on the character, and internal legitimacy, of their own institutions. Self-confident information takers with internal legitimacy can absorb flows of free information more readily, with less disturbance, than can institutions (governmental or nongovernmental) lacking such legitimacy and self-confidence.

Not all democracies are leaders in the information revolution; but as far as countries are concerned, most information shapers are democracies. This is not accidental. Their societies are familiar with the free exchange of information, and their institutions of governance are not threatened by it. They can shape information because they can also take it. Authoritarian states, typically among the laggards, have more trouble. At this point, governments such as the Republic of China can control the access of their citizens to the Internet by controlling Internet service providers and by monitoring the relatively small number of users. It is possible, but costly, to route around such restrictions, and control does not have to be complete to be effective for political purposes. Singapore has thus far combined its political controls with an increasing role for the Internet. However, as societies like Singapore reach levels of development at which a broader range of knowledge workers want fewer restrictions on access to the net, Singapore runs the risk of losing its scarcest resource for competing in the information economy. Thus Singapore today is wrestling with the dilemma of reshaping its education system to encourage the individual creativity that the information economy will demand and at the same time maintain existing social controls over the flow of information. Closed systems become more costly.

Closed systems also become more costly because it is risky for foreigners to invest funds in a country in which the key decisions are made in an opaque fashion. Transparency is becoming a key asset for countries seeking investments. The ability to keep information from leaving, which once seemed so valuable to authoritarian states, undermines the credibility and transparency necessary to attract investment on globally competitive terms. This point is illustrated by the Asian financial crisis. Governments that are not transparent are not credible, because the information they offer is seen as biased and selective. Moreover, as economic development progresses and middle-class societies develop, repressive measures become more expensive—not merely at home but also in terms of international reputation. Both Taiwan and South Korea discovered in the late 1980s that repression of rising demands for democracy and free expression would be expensive in terms of their reputation and soft power. By beginning to democratize then, they have strengthened their capacity—as compared with, for instance, Indonesia—to cope with economic crisis.

Whatever the future effects of interactivity and virtual communities, one political effect of increased flows of free information through multiple channels is already clear: states have lost much of their control over information about their own societies. States that seek to develop (with the exception of some energy suppliers) need foreign capital and the technology and organization that go with it. Geographic communities still matter most, but governments that want to see rapid development will find that they have to give up some of the barriers to information flows that have protected officials from outside scrutiny. No longer will governments that want high levels of development be able to afford the comfort of keeping their financial and political situations inside a national black box. The motto of the global information society might become, "If you can't take it, you can't shape it."

From a business standpoint, the information revolution has vastly increased the marketability and value of commercial information by reducing costs of transmission and the transaction costs of charging information users. Politically, however, the most important shift concerns free information. The ability to disseminate free information increases the potential for persuasion in world politics—as long as credibility can be attained and maintained. Nongovernmental organizations and other states can more readily influence the beliefs of people within other jurisdictions. If one actor can persuade others to adopt similar values and policies, whether or not it possesses hard power and strategic information may become relatively less important. Soft power and free information, if sufficiently persuasive, can change perceptions of self-interest and therefore the way hard power and strategic information are used. If governments or nongovernmental organizations are to take advantage of the information revolution, they will have to establish reputations for credibility in the world of white noise that constitutes the information revolution.

Conclusion

We are at such an early stage of the information revolution that any conclusions must be tentative. Nevertheless, current evidence supports three main arguments. First, the new conventional wisdom is wrong in its predictions of an equalizing effect of the information and communications revolutions on the distribution of power among states. This is in part because economies of scale and barriers to entry persist in regard to commercial and strategic information and in part because with respect to free information, the larger states will often be well placed in the competition for credibility. Second, cheap flows of information have created an order-of-magnitude change in channels of contact across state borders. Nongovernmental actors operating transnationally have much greater opportunities to organize and to propagate their views. States are more easily penetrated and less like black boxes. Political leaders will find it more difficult to maintain a coherent ordering of foreign policy issues. Third, the information revolution is changing political processes in such a way that soft power becomes more important in relation to hard power than it was in the past. Credibility becomes a key power resource both for governments and nongovernmental organizations, giving more open, transparent organizations an advantage with respect to free information. Although the coherence of government policies may diminish in more pluralistic and penetrated states, those same countries may be better placed in terms of credibility and soft power. In short, geographically based states will continue to structure politics in an information age, but the processes of world politics within that structure are undergoing profound change.

Notes

1. Norman Angell, *The Great Illusion: A Study of the Relation of Military Power in Nations to Their Economic and Social Advantage* (London: Heinemann, 1911).

2. Robert O. Keohane and Joseph S. Nye, *Power and Interdependence: World Politics in Transition* (Boston: Little, Brown, 1977), p. 4.

Contributors

All contributors, except where noted, are at the John F. Kennedy School of Government, Harvard University

Arthur Isak Applbaum
Professor of Ethics and Public Policy

Jane E. Fountain
Associate Professor of Public Policy

William A. Galston
Professor, School of Public Affairs, University of Maryland, and Director, Institute for Philosophy and Public Policy

Elaine Ciulla Kamarck
Lecturer in Public Policy

Robert O. Keohane
James B. Duke Professor of Political Science, Duke University

David C. King
Associate Professor of Public Policy

Jerry Mechling
Lecturer and Director, E-Government Executive Education Project

Pippa Norris
Associate Director for Research and Lecturer, Joan Shorenstein Center on the Press, Politics and Public Policy

Joseph S. Nye Jr.
Don K. Price Professor of Public Policy and Dean of the John F. Kennedy School of Government

Dennis Thompson
Alfred North Whitehead Professor of Political Philosophy and Director, University Center for Ethics and the Professions

179

Index